Total Leaders 2.0

Leading in the Age of Empowerment

Charles J. Schwahn and William G. Spady

Published in partnership with the
American Association of School Administrators

ROWMAN & LITTLEFIELD EDUCATION
A division of
ROWMAN & LITTLEFIELD PUBLISHERS, INC.
Lanham • New York • Toronto • Plymouth, UK

Published in partnership with the American Association of School Administrators

Published by Rowman & Littlefield Education
A division of Rowman & Littlefield Publishers, Inc.
A wholly owned subsidary of The Rowman & Littlefield Publishing Group, Inc.
4501 Forbes Boulevard, Suite 200, Lanham, Maryland 20706
www.rowmaneducation.com

Estover Road, Plymouth PL6 7PY, United Kingdom

British Library Cataloguing in Publication Information Available

Library of Congress Cataloging-in-Publication Data

Schwahn, Charles J.
   Total leaders 2.0 : leading in the age of empowerment / Charles J. Schwahn and William G. Spady.
      p. cm.
   "Published in partnership with the American Association of School Administrators."
   Includes bibliographical references.
   ISBN 978-1-60709-530-9 (cloth : alk. paper) — ISBN 978-1-60709-531-6 (pbk. : alk. paper) — ISBN 978-1-60709-532-3 (electronic)
   1. School management and organization. 2. Educational leadership. 3. Educational change. I. Spady, William G. II. American Association of School Administrators. III. Title.
   LB2805.S443 2010
   371.2—dc22   2009050116

Printed in the United States of America

CONTENTS

PREFACE

We were honored when, in 1997, we were asked by the American Association of School Administrators to write a book on the topic of leadership. The initial success of *Total Leaders* took us a bit by surprise, and we felt a deep sense of gratitude to our AASA colleagues for their support—and, of course, for buying the book. We were also a bit surprised with the continued success of *Total Leaders* over the past decade, and again feel honored to have been asked to update our work in this form—*Total Leaders 2.0: Leading in the Age of Empowerment*. It has been a good ride, and we are humbled and appreciative.

When we received the invitation late in 2008 to update *TL*, and after recovering somewhat from the feelings of satisfaction and joy, we realized that we needed to answer a couple of very important questions: Should we do it? And if so, what form should the "sequel" take? You now have *TL2.0* in your hands, so we obviously chose to do it. But *TL2.0* is more a new book than an update, more a fresh and deep look at leadership than a second edition. We have retained the tried-and-true, the TL framework, but more than half of *TL2.0* is "new, improved, and more filling."

Chapters 1 and 2 will help you identify today's realities, the exciting and challenging context in which you are asked/required to lead. Chapter 1 is about the new U.S. culture of empowerment and the technological tools that drive it. Chapter 2 is about our global challenges—global, but in today's world, global is also local. Leaders everywhere are impacted by worldwide shifts and trends, and they must be paying attention.

Chapter 3 is about what has happened to "leadership" over the past decade. Leadership, future-focusing, change, and deep inner character are no longer four distinct topics; they are "joined at the hip." Chapter 4 reintroduces the TL framework that is at the heart of our work and takes you on our trip of the past ten years—what we have learned and how our leadership thinking has expanded and deepened. We're both uncontrolled lifelong learners who love learning about the art and science of leadership from our favorite and famous leadership gurus.

Chapters 5, 6, and 7 get specific about the five leadership domains, the change pillars, and the critical performance roles of the TL2.0. The "what and the how" of leadership is contained therein . . . all based on our synthesis of what today's fifty-plus most respected leadership gurus—those researchers, authors, and consultants who fill the leadership section of your favorite bookstore—have taught us.

But other people have given these two books their titles. When we submitted *Total Leaders* for publication back in 1997, we had titled our manuscript *Holistic Leadership*. Our AASA editor suggested that the title should be *Total Leaders* instead. A brilliant move! Clear, powerful, descriptive, a bit arrogant, and "sticky"—as in, easy to remember and to say. We owe her big time.

The title *Total Leaders 2.0* for this work was suggested by Bea McGarvey, a longtime friend and colleague. *TL2.0* fits neatly because the book is a second version of a future-focused book that recognizes and rides the impact that technology continues to have on our leadership world. We think the title rings and rhymes with the spirit and content of our work. Our subtitle, "Leading in the Age of Empowerment," identifies and communicates one of the most dynamic megatrends of today's society. We believe that the information age didn't change how organizations operated or how leaders led as much as it changed the speed and power of decisions and actions.

However, today's age of empowerment—brought on by a new culture in which people expect meaningful work, expect to be in control of their work life, expect to actualize their strengths and talents, think of themselves as "free agents" . . . and who are skilled with the transformational technology to accommodate all of the above—has flipped and flattened organizational charts nearly everywhere. Organizations, people's expectations and opportunities, and leadership will never again be the same. Today's formula for success is: meaningful work + access to information + creativity + empowerment = innovation and productivity.

Our aims for *Total Leaders 2.0: Leading in the Age of Empowerment* are bold. In a short, easy-to-read (we think so, anyway) book, we expect to

- Provide a clear and comprehensive definition of leadership, one that would have the approval of nearly all leadership gurus of the day

- Create a common professional leadership vocabulary for your leadership team and foster a continuous professional dialogue that facilitates the development of all present and future leaders

- Equip you with a brief yet comprehensive leadership framework (you might think of it as a model) that will serve as a place-holder for all of your leadership attitudes, beliefs, ideas, skills, experiences, and new learning

- Supply you with the most authoritative "CliffsNotes" for trans-formational leadership, change processes and strategies, and future-focusing—creating "you, the leadership expert" in less than one hundred fifty pages

- Support each of you as you become a more authentic and more effective leader . . . while having a significantly positive influence on your corner of the world

- Enlist you to be teachers and mentors of the next generation of TL2.0s

Our last aim is that you enjoy reading *TL2.0* as much as we have enjoyed putting it together. We strongly believe that our deepest learning comes when our biases and beliefs are tested—tested by those whom we trust and respect. So if you wish to be tested and to test a relationship, do a book with a respected, forthright friend and colleague. If you are courageous and candid enough, you'll be rewarded with immense personal and professional growth. Peter Drucker once wrote that he never learned much from reading, and that he learned most by writing. We agree with

St. Peter, of course . . . but then again, we don't think he ever had the opportunity to read *Total Leaders*.

Leadership is influence. Thanks for allowing us to influence you . . . and happy reading!

Chuck Schwahn
Bill Spady

CHAPTER ONE
WELCOME TO EMPOWERMENTLAND!

You have just entered Empowermentland! Welcome! It's an incredibly stimulating, exciting, and challenging place. And, if you pay close attention to what we're about to explore, you'll discover some things about our unfolding future that are sure to reshape your worldview, your sense of self, and how you see yourself as a leader in a world that just keeps on changing.

In fact, that's one of the interesting and exciting things about Empowermentland: Change is a constant—it just keeps happening, and rapidly, too. When we published *Total Leaders* in 1998, we did our best to describe the world of rapid and continuous change that leaders, their organizations, and their customers/clients/students faced. Like so many others at the time, we referred to it as the information age. Well, a lot has changed since then, and it embodies a giant leap forward into an era in which change is happening faster, wider, and deeper than the Total Leader of that day might have anticipated.

Our Evolving Age of Empowerment

And yes, you guessed it: Much of that change has been driven by an explosive evolution in the technologies available to most people in the "modern" world—technologies that have brought about a new era in human work, communications, economics, politics, relationships, creativity, and—yes—leadership. It's an era we view as the age of empowerment; hence, our visit to Empowermentland.

1

Why empowerment? Because empowerment is about people at whatever age intelligently and responsibly choosing and creating the life and future they want for themselves, irrespective of the limiting cultural, political, economic, religious, and educational institutions and orthodoxies that constitute their environment. It's about choice and being in control of the things that give life, work, and relationships real meaning and value. And humanity as a whole has never been in such an advantaged state.

There are countless millions more people across the planet today who are capable of and willing to exercise those options than even a decade or so ago. They have the education, the mind-set, the technologies, the motivation, and the opportunities to be the captain of their own ship—largely free of the serious cultural, political, geographic, and economic constraints that impeded their parents' and grandparents' generations not so long ago. And, unlike those older generations that were both culturally and psychologically tied to "We've got no choice," "That's just the way things are," and "We've always done it that way before," the tens of millions of future-shapers in the age of empowerment have exactly the opposite orientation. For them, it's "Since it's never been done before, let's try it. If it works, we've just invented the future!"—and, we would add, "we've just given humanity even more opportunities and choices than it had before."

So the "news" . . . and the message . . . in this chapter focuses on whether we're shaping the change we want to see, or simply reacting to what's happening around us. As empowered leaders, it's up to us to create the future we want to experience—and the educational system that will get us there. No one else is going to do it for us.

Becoming Future Focused

Just over two decades ago we became outspoken advocates of the notion that education badly needed to become future focused. By that we meant that continuing to pay lip service to the truism that "the purpose of education is to prepare students for the future" was not enough. That was rhetoric, but we were looking at practice. The world at that time—and, therefore, the future—was changing very rapidly, and in deep, fundamental ways. But from all we could see then, educational thinking and practice were falling farther and farther behind the leading-edge developments that were driving business and civic life across the modern world. We felt what John Kotter's 2008 book calls a sense of urgency, and our position on this was clear from the outset:

- Education needs to redefine, reframe, and retool itself *explicitly* around the future challenges, opportunities, problems, and conditions that its students are extremely likely to encounter once they leave the institution.

Otherwise it cannot claim to be preparing them for the rapidly evolving future they inevitably face.

Both to support our position and assist our clients, in 1987 we began tracking and summarizing the range of insights being offered by the leading futurists of the day regarding the shifts and trends of significance that were then emerging. We named our initial analysis of these trends "The Future IS Now." And because these shifts, trends, and conditions are where the "rubber" of leadership meets the ever-changing "road" of life, we've been updating and highlighting that document regularly ever since. For it provides us with an unfolding snapshot of what we educators must attend to in preparing our young people for that dynamic future.

Hence, we're inviting you here to step into our future-focused perspective . . . to explicitly focus and ground your thinking on the existing and emerging conditions that define the age of empowerment, just like successful leaders in business and industry do. The more you do this, the better you'll be able to use that information to design and implement the learning experiences (which we commonly call "curriculum") that your young people will have—experiences that will directly, not just indirectly, equip them with the understandings and skills to (1) anticipate, (2) deal with, (3) thrive in the face of, and (4) proactively improve the conditions that prevail in today's and tomorrow's world. And once you start thinking like a futurist, you can take the next step: keeping your fellow educators, students, parents, and constituents aware of and focused on the powerful "big picture" shifts and trends occurring in Empowermentland.

What's Happening in Empowermentland

Here's a cross-section of several major things that are deeply affecting our lives in the early part of the twenty-first century—who we are, how we view

the world, how we function, and our opportunities for success and fulfillment in the years ahead. For starters, everywhere you look things are . . .

Faster, Better, Smaller, Cheaper

Don't blink, or you might miss something! The world's a little faster
than you think. We all feel the speed of today's world—and some of us,
for good reason, wish it would slow down. Well, don't count on it, at least
as far as technology is concerned.

Transformational Technologies: Approaching Warp Speed

Technology is bigger and more powerful than a "trend." It is the force
impelling most of the other conditions described here. Actually, technological breakthroughs have happened so fast in the past decade, they no
longer shock and amaze us. We've come to expect them. The real surprise
for us, then, is not about how fast innovations come at us, but *how deeply
they change the way we live.*

Way back in the information age, technology made us more efficient at
what we normally did. We could transact business faster, more accurately,
and with less energy. But today's technologies are transformational—they're
changing the very structure of organizations, processes, and people's lives.
Think iPhone: If you own one you may not have to take your laptop.
(Laptop? Twenty years ago they were more vision than reality, but today
"everyone" has one and can't live without it—unless, of course, they own an
iPhone!) Or think Amazon.com: They're not only selling more than books
online, they're selling Kindles, which are making books obsolete!

Moreover, these versatile handheld telephones/televisions/comput-
ers/cameras/entertainment centers/storage devices/communications tools
that we carry around (in the color and style of our choice) were absolutely
unimaginable a few decades ago. Now they are both "essential" and affordable to countless millions across the world. Yes, the famous "Moore's
law" is still clicking: The power of the microchip is doubling every eigh-
teen months, while getting cheaper and cheaper to buy. We're not only
carrying around its technological and financial benefits in our pockets, it's
also enabled us to gain control of our working lives and personal schedules
like never before.

Not long ago what we did was generally determined by our location (home, office, etc.), and we usually did one thing at a time in each place. Today, however, we seem to do a bit of everything everywhere—and all at once, too. Vince Poscente suggests in his book *The Age of Speed* that we should accept this blur and think of time as a tool that allows us to focus and act on our values and priorities, rather than simply on our location—just like "the empowered" do. So watch out: Technology is approaching warp speed and pulling everything else along with it!

Honey, They've Shrunk the World!

The past decade's new technologies have increased our range of interactions and our exchange of information, ideas, goods, and services beyond the wildest imaginations of most people just a few generations ago. What took months a century ago now takes hours, minutes, or even just seconds. Time zones, mountain ranges, and oceans have literally disappeared as limiting boundaries, and our work, family, and personal lives have changed profoundly as a result. The good news about living in this technology-rich, "anyone can connect with anyone else at any time from anywhere about anything" world we live in is that modernization has enabled more of us to get to know each other, share things, and get along better than ever before. As a result, the huge national, cultural, ethnic, language, religious, social class, economic, and sex-role differences/divisions/conflicts that have shaped human existence from its beginnings are definitely eroding. Some of the most dramatic recent evidence comes from the use of these technologies as individual Iranians reported to the world the extent of the protests against their government's manipulation of their presidential elections in June 2009—all in the face of an official news blackout. Tom Friedman's *The World Is Flat* became an instant classic in 2005, and its message concerning our global interconnectedness still rings clearly in today's globally interconnected world.

Look, Ma, I'm a Walking Encyclopedia!

If you own a laptop computer or an iPhone and have Internet access, you're a walking encyclopedia, and more! No more having to go to the library to look something up to impress your teachers, your mom, or your friends. If you know how to use it, you've got the entire knowledge base of modern man at your fingertips, and you can do just about anything from anywhere at any time. And note, in some cases that knowledge base is being updated hourly. If this isn't proof that we're in the age of empowerment, we don't know what is.

But what about textbooks and curriculum standards? They're archaic! And so is memorizing things for Friday's test. The empowered think Google—as in, "Just a second, I'll Google that!"—and they quickly become the smartest person in their organization or the smartest kid in their class. Oh, and don't forget the news: up to the minute, with photos, on any topic you want (and with any slant or bias you prefer), sent from across the world . . . often from someone's iPhone! What's important to develop, then, is the ability to access and sift through all the information on Google or Wikipedia and discern what's credible, useful, and has deeper meaning for your life—and that takes critical thinking and good judgment, not just flashing fingers.

Our 24/7 Existence

The good news is that today's transformational technologies are giving their empowered users an astonishing degree of flexibility any time of any day they want to use them. For example, many business transactions are "friction-free"—they require no humans, and no one has to touch anything. Electronic technology takes care of everything. In that case, why not be open for business 24/7? You may remember that until ATMs came along, most banks were only open from 9 a.m. to 3 p.m. ". . . for your banking inconvenience." But now, except for getting your weekly supply of twenties, you don't even have to go to an ATM . . . you do it all from home, online, in your jam-jams, at 11 p.m. while sipping your favorite nightcap. Moreover, businesses now know that empowered customers have choices; they wisely compare products and services and go where they find both value and convenience. And convenience means being open and ready for business when the "customer as king" has needs, which is usually after "normal" business hours. For many, 24/7 goes well beyond the economy. It's about life: communication, relationships, news, work, and entertainment.

Nanotech and Biotech Breakthroughs

Nanotech and biotech have become buzzwords and major forces in the arenas of health, medicine, and food production. And, in the process, they have become a significant part of the world economy. Dolly, the cloned sheep, and the assembly of the human genome sequence are milestones of great significance in what promises to be an age of amazing biotechnology breakthroughs. Food as medicine is on the near horizon, and the good news for couch potatoes, who spend their sedentary lives in front of one kind of screen or another, is that scientists at the University of California, Berkeley, are building devices—nanomotors, if you will—with the ability to clean human arteries. So don't be surprised when it's announced that stents or serious surgery are no longer needed to clear arteries that have been clogged from the prolonged consumption of junk food, or that cloning has moved from Dolly to Don or Donna.

But the other side of this coin is the vocal resistance of some empowered consumers to purchasing or eating genetically engineered anything. Anticipate a pitched battle between those who see biotech and nanotech as solutions to our world's basic problems and those who see them as a threat to the environment and all life forms, including us.

Redefining "Normal" Life Cycles

Have you noticed that the definition of "normal" is changing? In many aspects of our lives, it is now normal to be . . . well . . . not so normal. Lives used to be relatively short, linear, and predictable. Youth was for school, education came just once, adult life was for work and family, marriage lasted a lifetime, retirement was at sixty-five, and death would come . . . well, pretty soon after that. Not only could savvy marketers predict what your age group would buy, but psychologists could predict your attitudes and priorities, and fashion designers could tell women what they'd be wearing. But today's lives are lived in cycles. Most young adults will have three or four different careers and hold about a dozen different jobs. Education happens whenever, not just in your pre-adult years, and children can come late in life. Basically, anyone in Empowermentland can spin off the linear path at any time and "do their own thing," plan their life on the fly, and be accepted and rewarded by society for doing it.

Quality and Success Are Transitory

Because of both the speed of technological change and the intensity of global competition, today's "state-of-the-art" product or service can quickly become next month's "also-ran." While quality products and services were once a distinct market advantage, they are simply taken for granted today. Hence, greatness and success are fleeting, and the faster things move and the more access to new information we have, the more fleeting they are. While the timeline for something going from "innovation" status to "commodity" status used to be about three to five years, that timeline has now shrunk to months. And, on the very day you release it, you can be sure that someone else out there is copying every good aspect of it and figuring out how to produce something just a bit better, and for less.

That's why smart companies innovate while on top rather than trying to ride the crest of the wave of their new success for very long. Customers want things quick, want them to work well, want to be the first on their block to have them, *and* want them to be designed with class and elegance. Think Apple Inc. and the iPod, iPhone, and MacBook Air—classy design is the new difference. If you hear "We've always done it this way before" in Empowermentland, you know it means "Expect our going-out-of-business sale any time now!"

Mass Customization

Segments of the global market are pressing for products and services that meet highly specific needs. Nimble organizations find ways of anticipating and meeting individual needs quickly on a mass scale. Advanced technologies in the hands of adept employees achieve the mass customization necessary for capturing and sustaining viable markets for their organization's products and services.

Meeting unique customer needs is more a matter of profiling customers and managing information in a timely manner than maintaining large inventories of tangibles. Prime examples: Amazon.com can customize service to its more than three million customers daily. Starbucks keeps that line moving even when every other person seems to be ordering "an extra hot venti chai latte, no fat, no foam, no water." Dell Computer manufactures eighty thousand customized computers per day and has a storage area for inventory that is 10' by 10'—an area smaller than your guest bedroom. Pandora.com allows you to create a radio station that plays your favorite music, all for free. And, of course, Google already knows what you will want to know.

Power to the Empowered

The age of empowerment requires both individuals and organizations to be future focused, technologically adept, risk-takers, capable of rapid and continuous change, light on their feet, and constantly learning and improving. Those who embody this kind of forward-looking self-direction become invaluable assets to their communities and organizations, since their talents may spell the difference between an organization thriving or going out of business. And despite the economic downturn of 2008–2009, power has shifted from the company to the talented, creative, responsible employee who loves challenge and knows how to create and expand opportunities. Because these employees are in demand, smart leaders treat them with respect, provide them the flexibility they want, give them control, and ensure that they find meaning in their work—or lose them to another company or to the "free agent" entrepreneur pool that continues to grow in this era of ever-expanding talent, creativity, opportunity, and choice.

But empowerment has reached the individual consumer level, too. Note that every time you go online to purchase a product, you find it rated by all the previous consumers . . . and you even find their ratings summarized and rated as well. Hence, as we noted in *Total Leaders*, the customer is king, and technology has reinforced that reality in the intervening decade. A fun and thought-provoking read on this general topic is Timothy Ferriss's *The Four-Hour Workweek*. For a more scholarly look, go to *Five Minds for the Future*, by Howard Gardner.

Empowered People Produce

Empowerment works! It's not just a buzzword, and it's here to stay! Empowerment is about self-direction. It honors the intrinsic motivation of people to use their experience and expertise to best advantage and gives them a direct stake in achieving success in all aspects of their lives—personal, career, social, and political—and a genuine sense that they "really matter" and can "make a difference" in the larger scheme of things. It comes as no surprise, then, that smart businesses give qualified people control over their work. Why? Because it's both morally right and financially profitable, especially when the empowered get a piece of the financial action!

And, as you'll see in chapter 4, empowerment works best when employees (1) deeply identify with organizational purpose; (2) have a clear vision of where the organization wants to go; (3) have a strong commitment to getting there; (4) have the information, capabilities, and tools to get there; and (5) receive the organizational supports necessary for accomplishing its vision. You guessed it: Creating those five conditions is the Total Leader's main job!

Competence as Capital, Knowledge as Power

The knowledge and technology explosions have also changed the nature of work and the determinants of organizational success. Today, most organizations' greatest assets are not their bricks, mortar, and equipment, but their people's expertise, creativity, and commitment. That's why attracting, developing, and utilizing competent, growth-oriented staff—or buying companies with exceptional staff capacity and promise—have replaced the accumulation of capital as an organization's best assurance of staying competitive. And if you don't have talent and the ability to think analytically and creatively, don't expect to last in the pressure cooker of big business. That's why economic survival and business success are increasingly about people—about attracting talent, empowering talent, rewarding talent, and, hopefully, retaining talent. And since talent is empowered and mobile, it has opened the door to . . .

Free Agency and the Anywhere, Anytime Workplace

Like it or not, lifetime loyalty to a single organization is a thing of the past, because the entrepreneurial spirit—another expression of empowerment—is blossoming as individuals choose to go it on their own. As many as thirty-three million Americans may be free agents today, selling their services, expertise, and advice to multiple clients. Free agents come in many forms: temps, consultants, freelancers, proprietors of home-based businesses, and other self-selected labels. They are trading security for freedom, opportunity, authenticity, and accountability. They move from job security to "jobless security" by making every day count while embodying quality, entrepreneurship, passion, and professionalism at their best. Women and Generation Xers are leading the charge, and they often choose to blend rather than balance their personal lives, given that free agents can set their own schedules, and often work from anywhere. In response, organizations are more open than ever to flexible schedules, job-sharing, teaming arrangements, and offsite work—all of which emphasize worker autonomy, responsibility, and "getting the job done well" with minimum structure and supervision.

Mass Collaboration

Today's transformational technologies have deeply affected our social dynamics—and it's not just about text messaging! It has fostered a shift from the individual as hero to the synergistic and collaborative power of teams. While Web 1.0 was for the "point and click" generation like us, Web 2.0 provides free, open-source tools such as Apache (Web server), Linux (operating system), MySQL (database application), Mozilla/Firefox (browser), and PHP (programming language) that allow people to interact, collaborate, and contribute to joint products and solutions—all online and in real time. Anyone with the requisite skills to participate in the conversation can be a real player.

Major corporations use this virtual environment and these free, open-source tools to build customer loyalty and coalitions of collaborators who provide them with solutions. So did both major U.S. political parties in the 2008 elections, and in doing so they drew levels of mass participation beyond what we'd seen before. Look at Clay Shirky's *Here Comes Everybody* for a deeper look at this emerging phenomenon; and check out *Wikinomics* by Don Tapscott and Anthony Williams for the full story of how Web. 2.0 has transformed communication and collaboration.

The Feminine Factor

Although cultural stereotypes die hard, the United States has experienced the feminine factor in the past century, and it has changed every fabric of our society—business, politics, education, religion, marriage, and family relationships. We think of it as female empowerment, and we were reminded of how far it has come in the presidential candidacy of Hillary Clinton in 2008. (A century earlier, women weren't even allowed to vote.) And you have a paradigm shift of gigantic proportions when you consider the large proportion of new businesses that are owned and operated by women and the growing numbers of women who head large corporations, hold major academic positions, conduct symphony orchestras, run school districts, and exhibit stellar performances in athletic competitions of all kinds.

In addition, women represent a new, congenial, relationship-oriented approach to leadership that balances the command-and-control approach so widely accepted in traditional male-dominated firms and pursuits. According to Tom Peters's book *Re-Imagine!* "Women get it!" They naturally get relationships, teaming, cooperation, and networking when organizations badly need . . . well . . . relationships, teaming, cooperation, and networking—something we'll explore more in chapter 4!

Conscious Empowerment

Have you noticed that the "C" word is creeping into our mainstream vocabulary? And its meaning is expanding, too. "Conscious" no longer means just being awake, out of bed, and aware of what's going on. It's coming to mean being *deeply* awake, with your inner eyes wide open, and aware of what's going on—looking and probing beneath the surface appearance of things for their deeper essence, meaning, and potential. And not just intellectually either, though that's a part of it. The emerging "new consciousness movement" in the Western world is rooted in a deep exploration of our remarkable spiritual nature and the countless outside-the-box possibilities that open to us as a consequence.

Ask any major bookstore which section has expanded the most during the past decade, and you'll get an answer that reflects people's desire for inner growth, self-improvement, and more "conscious," "natural," "healthful," and "holistic" ways of living. That search is taking more people both "deeper within" themselves and "farther beyond" our conventional, rational, three-dimensional worldview than ever before. Their desire: to expand their inner awareness, reduce stress, and enhance health—and with the blessing of the Mayo Clinic to boot, which recommends that you "nurture your spirit, no matter what you call your source of inspiration," in order to improve your physical and mental well-being.

The Oprah Effect

Oprah Winfrey has gotten rich and famous during the past decade by promoting authors and "teachers" whose work focuses on activating humanity's enormous but largely untapped inner potential. Did you hear the buzz about her watershed event of 2008? It was her online course with Eckhart Tolle on his book *A New Earth*. Over twelve million viewers registered, read the book, and involved themselves in discussing its consciousness-expanding, paradigm-shifting messages. Then add to her visibility and influence the prodigious sales of "consciousness-raising" books and workshops by Gregg Braden, Deepak Chopra, Wayne Dyer, Esther Hicks, Barbara Marx Hubbard, Byron Katie, Tom Kenyon, James Twyman, Neale Donald Walsch, Marianne Williamson, and Gary Zukov (among a host of others), and you have an irreversible cultural movement going.

Regulating the Reckless

Nothing gets your attention like watching your home value and life savings plummet in a few weeks' time. That happened in September and October of 2008, and it got everyone's attention—worldwide! As the revelations emerged, the magnitude of the crisis surfaced, and the causes were explored, there was a mega-shift in perspective about "free"-market—some say "greed-driven"—economics and humanity's love affair with materialism and status symbols. Accompanying this shift was widespread outrage that a relative handful of individuals could/would so willingly manipulate so much money at the expense of so many others. And the outrage multiplied as the CEOs of failing financial institutions maneuvered to keep themselves in line to continue receiving multimillion-dollar salaries and bonuses, while everyone else's assets were devaluing and/or disappearing by the hour. The good news is that it woke people up and made them demand accountabilities of all kinds in our public and private institutions. The bad news became the daily headlines for many months afterward.

CHAPTER ONE

Living Frugally

The economic crisis of 2008–2009 had another beneficial "awakening" effect that had begun a couple of decades earlier among America's growing population of senior citizens: downsizing and simplifying! More and more older people were already realizing that they no longer needed all of the material things they'd been accumulating throughout their adult years, and they had cut back enormously—selling their large homes, much of their furniture, their extra cars, and so on, with the desire to live happily on, and with, less. Countless others had this "opportunity" thrust upon them by the crisis, and they too learned that "less" meant survival and "more" meant unmanageable indebtedness.

But those involved in the "new consciousness" movement came to appreciate a deeper and hidden benefit to the crisis, often expressed this way: "Just because it's customary or cool to have material possessions that bolster one's ego and presumably impress other people, impressing others isn't what my life is about. I'll do and choose things in my life with which I deeply resonate and that contribute to, and sustain, the well-being of life on this planet, period." Their mantra: "I am not my stuff!"

CHAPTER TWO
LIVING ON THE EDGE IN EMPOWERMENTLAND

It's easy to be dazzled and inspired by all of the advances described in chapter 1. But a very perceptive futurist named Robert Theobald reminded us back in 1987 that we were riding atop a swiftly moving current that he called the rapids of change—the flip side of what has become twenty-first-century "progress." Like riding the rapids in a fast-moving mountain river, there's no turning back. Everyone in the boat, Theobald argued—but especially the leader—had to be alert to eight major dangers that lay ahead, any one of which was ultimately powerful enough to spell catastrophe for humanity if we didn't collectively recognize and do something about them while there was still time. Just like the boulders and whirlpools in the river, we've known that these perils are there; but progress on addressing and averting them since 1987 has been slight.

Empowermentland's Rapids of Change

Therefore, it behooves us to address the shadow side of the conditions that are shaping our world—things that potentially threaten us in today's Empowermentland rapids. And, fortunately, there are books like Lester Brown's *Plan B 3.0: Mobilizing to Save Civilization* to help us stay on top of the rapids. Yes, it's going to take some exceptional collective vision, courage, skill, commitment, and leadership to address and avert them— but avert them we must. The quality of human existence and the planet's ability to sustain life are at stake. Watch out, and hold on tight!

Hello! The World Is Hot and Crowded, Too!

So states Tom Friedman in his 2008 sequel to *The World Is Flat*. Not only have advanced technologies, global markets, and transportation systems brought all of us closer together than ever before—the "flat" part—but there's a growing oversupply of "us" out there as well. And almost all of us want our "rightful" share of the material advancements that have defined "modernity" in recent decades. Then add to that all the air conditioners we'll need in an ever-warming global climate to sustain our "cool" expectations and lifestyles, plus the energy to operate them—causing even more pollution—and you begin to wonder how we, and the planet, are going to manage it all. Or can we? In *Hot, Flat, and Crowded*, Friedman goes a step beyond Theobald and suggests a host of specific things we can do to ward off this "perfect storm" of threatening conditions and preserve our quality of life. Put it on your must-read list now, and teach it to your students.

The Vulnerable Natural Environment

We've got tons of scientific evidence—depleting rainfall and water supplies in critical areas, melting icecaps, unprecedented dead zones in the ocean off our Pacific coastline, a brown cloud of dense pollution covering all of Asia, plus Al Gore's movie *An Inconvenient Truth*—to remind us that we have a global environmental crisis on our hands. And it will only get worse before it gets better, because we're still contributing to the problem while continuing to debate how much and when to cut back on our carbon emissions. The crisis involves not only "the greenhouse effect," rising temperatures, and climate change, but a depletion of the planet's oxygen supply as well—due to the unchecked cutting of rainforests in the earth's tropical zones and excessive logging in its temperate zones. Then, for dramatic effect, add the increased pollution of both our air and our streams and rivers that, among other things, results from ever-increasing factory production in the Third World—all of which ends up in our oceans and marine food supply. But wait, there's more! Enter . . .

The Population Bomb

So here we are—about six billion of us now—living in the same amount of space we had a century ago when there were only about a third as many of us around. And demographers tell us that this number is likely to double over the next forty years, with only 7 percent of that growth occurring in developed nations. If they're right, by 2050 there will be twelve billion of us, all wanting our fair share, or more, of the material resources we think we need to make life work for us—which quite directly means that we're going to depend on the planet, and each other, to provide us with those consumables. Given that the poor usually have more children than the rich in all countries, today's numbers tell a depressing story. Unless social consciousness, cultural norms, and economic conditions change radically, we're looking at a planet with an ever-increasing . . .

Maldistribution of Wealth and Opportunity

In almost every dimension of what we regard as quality of life and control over what influences one's life—the economic crisis of 2008–2009 notwithstanding—the Haves clearly have way more than the Have-Nots. And the odds are stacked hugely in favor of the Haves continuing to get even more of what the Have-Nots want, too. This is true at all levels of social organization everywhere: in local communities, in states, in nations, and globally. Whether it's the basics of existence, lifestyle consumables, access to quality health care and education, or a voice in the political process, the Haves not only now have *way more* than the Have-Nots, they also have the resources, capacity, and influence to continue having more of it! And since the potential for violent social and political revolution in a country is directly related to the gap between its richest and poorest people, the Have-Nots in many countries may have nothing to lose by trying to overthrow or eliminate the people and the system they believe are keeping them there.

The Voracious Modern Economy and Our Desire for "Stuff"

Modern life is driven by an economic engine (or paradigm) which assumes that production and consumption patterns can continue to expand endlessly. It's like a runaway train: More raw materials are extracted to produce more things for more people who take up more space and create more pollution of all kinds than the planet's ecosystem can ultimately handle. For obvious reasons, *The Rapids of Change* offers a compelling appeal to slow this engine down; but that will be difficult as long as the world's ever-expanding population remains "hooked on stuff." And not just the most basic kind—like clean air, safe water, affordable food, and shelter from the elements—but the stuff we acquire and consume to represent our status and importance in the world, the "latest and greatest" of everything out there: fancy cars, clothes, homes, and high-tech gadgets and "toys" of all kinds. And to acquire it, we've piled up mountains of debt along the way. If this issue rings your bell, check out the strategies for curbing our material excesses described in John Bogle's *Enough: True Measures of Money, Business, and Life.* And also get ahold of Daniel Goleman's latest book, *Ecological Intelligence.* It addresses this and the other key issues in this chapter in one comprehensive model.

Hurried, Harried, and Stressed

Can you spell "burnout"? Well, millions of Americans can, and it's showing up in all kinds of negative ways as people relentlessly pursue the good life. Deteriorating health, mounting personal debt, stressed relationships, and unmet family obligations head the list. We've been culturally conditioned to believe that we must continue to achieve and achieve in order to get ahead, but instead of helping us get there, all the amazing technologies we described earlier have simply allowed, or encouraged, us to do lots more in the same amount of time we always had. Remember the predictions that these technological marvels would shorten the average workweek in America and give us tons of leisure time? Well, instead, our working hours have expanded significantly. Americans are working 350 hours more per year than Europeans and even more than the industrious Japanese! And while the economic downturn of 2008–2009 put at least a temporary clamp on things, we've been trapped in a culture of consumerism in which buying things presumably creates the good life—which takes more money, which requires more work, which takes more time, which ultimately makes it harder to live the good life for which everyone's working so hard!

Hitting the "e-Addiction" Point

No addiction is healthy. In fact, addiction is the opposite of empowerment. The latter is about having constructive choices and exercising them. Addiction is a psychological dependence on something, accompanied by the feeling that you can't live without it. And that's where we've come in the modern world with "e"—to the point where our children are more preoccupied with e-games of all kinds than real ones. Gone for many is the spontaneity and joy of inventing and playing childhood games with friends—especially the active ones. Now the only things moving seem to be fingers, eyeballs, and mouths.

Yes, virtual reality simulations enable consumers to experience almost anything in detail from their homes, which they can purchase at their own convenience without ever having to go to a store. But kids' obsessions with video games is another matter, since psychologists fear that they're distorting healthy personal development and they're contributing seriously to our national epidemic of obese "e-couch potatoes." So ask yourself: Could your love affair with "e" be undermining the attention you give to more direct personal communication and relationships? Or do you spend as much time exercising your body as you do your keyboarding skills? Yes, we've become as perilously close to being "e-dependent" as we are "e-enhanced," and how to balance them isn't yet clear.

Living in Fear

As the brilliant futurist Joel Barker said two decades ago, "When a paradigm shifts, everyone goes back to zero." And zero is not a place where people want to go. Consequently, we all share an understandable fear of having what we've always known and relied on change in some unpredictable and threatening way, as it did for most of us in the economic downturn of 2008–2009. And the fear of not being either OK or safe or important makes us particularly vulnerable to manipulation.

The Western world's paradigm shifted on September 11, 2001, when the fear of continued attacks from terrorists began, and the fear message became imbedded in our media, politics, and daily lives. But the terrorists seem to be living in fear, too, abhorrent as their words and actions may be. It's the visceral fear of losing control of their religious culture as the "secular" and "materialistic" West threatens to undermine their traditional customs, beliefs, and what they interpret as the mandates of Allah/God. For them, violating these mandates spells eternal damnation in hell—which looks to be way worse than simply going back to zero in this lifetime! This is not an apology for their barbaric actions but an acknowledgment that, one way or another, we're all caught in the fear trap, and finding a way out isn't going to be easy, especially because of . . .

Humanity's Dominance Paradigm

Underlying most of the above is a deeply ingrained human paradigm that goes back to our earliest days as primates. Some know it as "eat or be eaten." Social scientists sometimes call it social Darwinism. Others call it dominance, competition, exploitation, superiority, or separation. In short, it's the fundamental psychological condition and orientation to life that is imbedded in our individual psyches, the teachings of most of our religions, the fabric of our cultures, and our relationship to the planet and other living creatures. We've been taught/conditioned to believe that to be safe and OK, we have to dominate something or someone by being better than they are in some way: stronger, smarter, faster, richer, "cooler," better educated, better looking, more famous, more influential, racially superior, believers in the right God, and so on. You name it, and we've got a better/worse rationale for it—not just unique and different, but superior and inferior! The comparisons come flying at us every day in the media, on the job, in our schools (grades and class rank), in our sports (we're number one), and in our social relationships.

If Bob Theobald were still with us, he might argue that *this* is the paradigm that must shift first in order for us to safely navigate the other rapids of change. But in the meantime, cultures, religions, ethnic groups, and political systems across the world continue to claim superiority over others—which clearly encourages . . .

Paradigm Clashes on a Global Scale

There are lots of other paradigms competing for attention and dominance in our social, political, economic, and religious lives, too. They can be found defining everything from our individual thinking and actions to the values underlying our global institutions. Each carries its definition of right/wrong, true/false, and better/worse—and each has been and continues to be the reason used to justify humanity's millennia of struggles, conflicts, and wars.

For example, consider the expansionism-sustainability rift; that is, the believers in "more and bigger is better" versus the "we can't keep expanding and consuming like this" folks. Or how about the separation-unity divide, with the "we are all separate and distinct individuals" people versus the "we are all one physical and spiritual family" believers? And if that doesn't sufficiently get your attention, try the theocracy-secularism conflict, with the "God demands that everyone live like this" advocates versus the "each is free to choose what to believe and how to live" people. (Notice how dramatically this one played out in the Iranian election protests of June 2009.) Woven throughout these previous three divisions, of course, is the ever-present modernity–tradition struggle—frequently, but not always, imbedded in a kind of generational divide between the young who "love anything new and exciting" and the old who "revere the familiar ways of the past." Cutting across virtually all of these conflicts is the opportunity-privilege battle, the ultimate source of humanity's fixation on winners and losers, and the spoils that go with being the winner. And regardless of who "wins," it usually leaves the losers aching for revenge and retribution, further fueling the struggle, often for centuries, with no end in sight.

Education's Empowerment Dilemma

You don't have to be a trend-tracking specialist to realize that there have been two dominant trends in education over the past decade or so that are profoundly contradictory. One is the "standards" movement; the other is the "exodus" movement. For us, the key implication of life in Empowermentland for education is that

> Anyone can learn anything at anytime from anywhere from world-class experts using the most transformational technologies and resources available to enhance their personal interests and life fulfillment.

Now contrast that with what has been education's prevailing template for the past century:

- Specific students of a specific age must learn specific things on a specific schedule in a specific classroom from a specific teacher using specific materials and methods so that they can pass specific tests on specific dates—and only then be called "OK."

The latter embodies a structure and culture of control, standardization, constraint, and compliance. This system determines what is to be done to whom, by whom, and when. Flexibility of any kind can only be gained by "working the system" at its margins whenever possible. As we'll describe in much more detail in chapter 1 of *Learning Communities 2.0*, this way of educating can rightfully be called "school in a box," and its nature is fundamentally and profoundly "assembly-line" and industrial age.

And now for the really bad news: Today's standards movement is simply reinforcing all of the constraints and rigidities of this assembly-line approach! The who, what, when, where, why, and how of education are being even more stringently determined by these external political mandates, and a serious exodus movement has begun. Who's leaving? Just read the headlines, or look around:

- Students who find it impossible to meet the standards

- Educators who find the rigidities and narrow approach unbearable

- Parents in huge numbers who are seeking a better, more enlightened, humane, learner-responsive approach for their children

That's why the terms home schooling, vouchers, and charter schools are now commonplace.

Yes, some of this exodus has been motivated by less than noble motives—attempts to escape from racial or language minority groups, and/or overt attempts to privatize the system for corporate profit. But as we noted when describing the Oprah effect, adults who are sensitive to their own inner selves and unique potentials know the vast array of gifts and qualities we humans possess, and their lives exemplify their desire for more and deeper exploration and development of these capacities. From their perspective, the only kind of education that is suitable for their children—or any children, for that matter—encourages, embraces, and directly supports the development of each child's unique interests, motivations, and gifts.

And while they are convinced that this is *not* achievable in the system of impersonal standardization that education embodies today, they believe it *is* achievable through a variety of more progressive, experiential, and learner-centered approaches. This certainly helps explain why most Montessori schools and Waldorf schools in the United States are bursting at the seams, and why flexibly structured "alternative schools" of various kinds are gaining a foothold across the country. For a deeper read on these issues and the empowering alternatives available to local schools, see Spady's *Beyond Counterfeit Reforms* and carefully study what's described in *Learning Communities 2.0*.

CHAPTER THREE
LEADERSHIP, CHANGE, AND CHARACTER: JOINED AT THE HIP

We've just seen that success in our modern world is transitory, largely because change is fast, deep, continuous, and often dramatic. That's why organizations that are not changing, and changing in the right direction faster than the speed of change in the society that surrounds them, are most likely on a downhill spiral and in the process of going out of business.

Consequently, today's successful leaders must know change, must accept change, must embrace change, must welcome change, and (it might be a stretch, but) maybe they actually have to love change, its challenges, and its excitement. Simply put, leaders lead change. Their real name should be "changeleaders"! They are trusted and courageous future-focused visionaries who involve everyone in the change process, who develop and empower everyone, and who provide personal and organizational support for vision-driven change. While these fundamentals remain as true today as when we wrote *Total Leaders* twelve years ago, leadership has had to become even more dynamic, yet firmly grounded, as the pace and depth of change has accelerated.

Leadership and Change: New Definitions and New Thinking

That's why leadership has changed dramatically with the acceleration of change. In the olden days of stability and security, the terms "leadership" and "management" were thought to be almost synonymous. Today the two terms refer to significantly different attitudes, behaviors, and responsibilities. The consensus among today's leadership gurus is that leadership is about doing the right thing, and management is about doing things right; leadership is about vision and direction-setting, and management is about organizing and coordinating; leadership is about meaning and motivation, and management is about supervision and accountability. Everyone agrees that both leadership and management are very important, but they are also very different; they require different outlooks, different attitudes, different talents, and different skills.

In his bestseller *The One Thing You Need to Know*, Marcus Buckingham, one of the new and respected gurus of the day, suggests that people can be quite good at both leadership and management, but they must know when they are doing one or the other. He suggests that effective managers "discover what is unique about each person and capitalize on it," while leaders "discover what is universal and capitalize on it." Both are important, but they are not interchangeable. When you want to manage, you start with the person. When you want to lead, you begin with a vision—you begin with a clear picture of where you're headed and what getting there will look like.

Buckingham, who backs his positions with a wealth of relevant data and research, is one of the leading advocates of what is frequently labeled the "strengths movement." Basically, it advocates acknowledging the unique talents of people and working with those strengths to help them become more productive, more engaged, and more successful. The converse, and widely accepted approach, is to focus on people's weaknesses and to go about "fixing" them so that they perform in a more "balanced" way. The leadership literature of the past ten years or so generally supports Buckingham's approach. In fact, Tom Rath, coauthor of the bestselling *Strengths-Based Leadership*, boldly states, "If you spend your life trying to be good at everything, you will never be great at anything." So, yes, the "strengths movement" is gaining momentum, and here's a "bottom line" about its essence that you can post on your office wall:

> Motivation and productivity, no matter what the field or what the level of creativity, are significantly enhanced when we use our strongest talents

while creating and producing something that has intrinsic meaning and really engages us.

Key Character Components: Passion and Optimism

And here's another:

> If you are continuously or even frequently negative and pessimistic, you have a moral obligation to leave your leadership position. The people you are supervising deserve better!

This one was made by a Total Leader—a person who's a school superintendent and a leader of leaders. And it was made with emotion, passion, and more than a few decibels, we would add. Buckingham would agree with her. While most leadership scholars tend to believe that leadership can be taught and learned by everyone, Buckingham does not. His data support the point, and we'll address that in a moment.

But first, we need to place a large part of this chapter in a proper context and give credit where it is most due: to Daniel Goleman and his powerful, multifaceted concept known as emotional intelligence (EQ). From one perspective, the EQ label is itself a "construct"—a concept that is made up of multiple parts. There are at least three of them—one is about one's "inner" presence of mind and self-management of thoughts and emotions; the other two are about how that translates into relating to the world and other people. Most educators are familiar with Goleman's original book, *Emotional Intelligence*, but we've discovered that his second, *Working with Emotional Intelligence*, makes an even more powerful case for how critical EQ is to career and leadership success and advancement. If you haven't seen it, it's absolutely worth the read.

And, without getting tangled up in all the esoterica of personality psychology, we want to highlight here the central role that EQ plays in the range of things we're calling "character." Why? Because character lies at the core of leadership performance and effectiveness, and character takes in a broad range of EQ-related things—like personality traits, innate abilities, learning styles, paradigm thinking, core values and principles, temperament, adaptability, and so forth.

So with EQ and character firmly emblazoned on our leadership banner, let's move ahead and consider a key character trait: optimism. We've learned that effective leaders are optimists, and our friend Buckingham believes optimism can't be taught. Most people can learn to be good managers, because managing is about an attitude and a skill set. But leadership is about vision, optimism, and bringing a can-do approach to both leadership and life that resides deep within our psyche. Optimism is something we are born or blessed with, but it is not really taught or learned.

Well, yes, natural pessimists can all probably be optimistic about some things for a short time. But over the stretch, negative/pessimistic people will tend to be negative and pessimistic, and positive and optimistic people will tend to be positive and optimistic. If you're born with an optimism meter set at 3, you may at times find that, when all is well, your meter jumps to 5. But when the new "feel good" becomes the norm, the meter returns to 3. (Remind us to tell you the one about the pessimistic little boy who is given a horse for Christmas while his optimistic twin brother is given a room full of horse manure. Call if you haven't figured out the punch line.)

What might you expect if your passion and optimism intersected with your talents, competencies, and skills? Ken Robinson, in his popular book *The Element: How Finding Your Passion Changes Everything*, challenges us all to discover our passion and to identify our talents and competencies that intersect with that passion. From his perspective, when your passion aligns with your natural talents, you are in "the element"—quite similar to what Joseph Jaworski calls synchronicity. Think of Michael Jordan in his NBA championship games. Or think of Dr. Martin Luther King making his "I Have a Dream" speech. When we are in the element, in the zone, in the flow, everything comes easy; we are in tune and alignment with our inner nature, we are productive, we are successful, and we are happy. Because they're very aware of their intrinsic gifts and motivators, Total Leaders are clear about their passion, optimistic about their vision, and skillful in carrying out the important performance roles that define Total Leadership.

The good news is that educational leaders get a running start when it comes to optimism and passion. Since education is arguably the most important and most meaningful of all professions, we have much going for us. If we can't get passionate about empowering learners to succeed in school and in life after school, what can we be passionate about?

Some Good Reads on Passion and Optimism

The Element: How Finding Your Passion Changes Everything by Ken Robinson. How to discover your passion and how to help others find theirs.

Now, Discover Your Strengths by Marcus Buckingham and Donald Clifton. If you are a fan of the "strengths movement," this is probably the bible.

The One Thing You Need to Know about Great Managing, Great Leading, and Sustained Individual Success by Marcus Buckingham. Note that Buckingham hits all of these topics with a research-based rationale that strongly supports the essence of the TL model . . . and it's an enjoyable read, too.

Key Character Components: Vision and Courage

We saw in chapter 1 that the "shelf life" of most ideas, innovations, and products is short. There was a time when a good product could ensure a strong market share for five years or more. Today, it's measured in months. Apple Inc. certainly ranks as an exemplar of foresight and innovation, and when the iPhone was introduced, they had the hottest electronic gizmo of the decade. But within weeks there were boasts from other companies that promised even more features and significantly cheaper prices. Yet would anyone doubt that Apple isn't already working on the next gizmo that will make the iPhone yesterday's buzz? Certainly they are! That's why successful twenty-first-century organizations that expect to remain successful become their own competition. The race is to see who makes their high-flying product obsolete first: they or their competitors?

Today it is hard to say "leadership" without also saying "vision" and "change." Productive change and continuous improvement can happen when leaders create exciting visions that "wow" customers and clients (think students, parents, communities here). Exciting and landscape-changing visions are shaped by fresh ideas that come from leaders who are students of the future, who keep their eyes on the horizon, and who have the ability to see around corners—almost like Clark Kent.

But TLs are future-focused visionaries who also have the courage to go for it. Why courage? Because leaders lead change, and change

29

is something that lots of their colleagues and constituents dread and resist—otherwise they would have already changed! Which is to say:

Leaders go where others fear to tread!

And they know that significant, productive change requires both having a vision of the possible (which, of course, hasn't happened yet) and the courage to step beyond the inertia of the times to make it happen. But note that courage without vision can be a loose cannon—kind of like being high on enthusiasm but low on accuracy. And vision without courage is wasted creativity—dreams that don't get translated into action and results, especially when the slope gets steep.

On balance, educators appear to have more skill than will in this regard. Education stands in stark relief to the continuously adapting organizations like Apple, described in chapter 1. As we'll describe in more detail in chapter 1 of *Learning Communities 2.0*, education is crying out for a vision that escapes its rigid, outdated, Industrial Age/assembly-line organizational structures—structures that (1) make it nearly impossible to implement strategies that resonate with and reflect what we know about human capacity, and (2) take advantage of what we know about how people learn. There seems to be no sense of urgency within the profession to transform and restructure these outdated and bureaucratic systems—an issue we'll be addressing forthrightly in our second book.

(This may be time for a bit of reflection, so please consider this: If productive change is not happening in your organization and in your area of responsibility, to what degree does it reflect a lack of leadership vision, and to what degree a lack of leadership courage? Be candid about this and see where your viewpoint leads you.)

Transformational Technology and the Speed of Change

The speed and complexity of change has definitely had a significant impact on leadership. We are expected to lead at the speed of change, and many of the old ways of leading simply no longer work in today's fast-moving world. Other new forces and new realities are impacting the art and science of leadership.

For example, the old industrial age organizational chart was designed when people had to meet face-to-face to communicate effectively. The span of control (i.e., the number of people one could expect to supervise) ranged from eight to twenty or so, but usually was about a dozen. Those were the days of the large organizational pyramid, often with ten or more layers of leaders and managers. But today's information technology has reshaped the old pyramid to look more like a pancake—flat and thin. Supervision is now more a matter of forming problem-solving teams, monitoring productivity, and trying to meet the needs of talented and creative free agents. Following on our discussion in chapter 1, we use the term "free agents" rather than workers or employees because they must be treated with care lest they bolt for more dollars or for a work environment that allows them to bring their dog to work. (Here, think Google.)

Since *Total Leaders* came out in 1998, amazing advances in electronic technology have transformed not only how we communicate, how we entertain ourselves, and how we do business, but also how we lead. Leaders today have to understand the difference between technology that makes it easier to do something you're already familiar with and doing, and *transformational* technology. Transformational technology not only makes you better at what you do, it redefines/transforms how you do it. This is a key point for us educators, who mainly use computers to better do what we did pre-computer, like keep student records and schedule classes.

Had Amazon.com done that, they would have used new technology to better serve the needs of readers in brick-and-mortar buildings. But Amazon transformed the industry of book selling by selling books online and profiling readers so that they could make customized recommendations for future reads. Moreover, they transformed the basic *processes* for selling books. And they did it with about one-tenth the staff required to sell an equivalent number of books in a traditional bookstore.

But they didn't stop there. With the new Kindle 2 (a gizmo not much larger than a small tablet that can hold 1,500 books—yes, that's one thousand, five hundred), Amazon has again leapfrogged the rest of the industry and now delivers "books?" to your specific location—any location in the United States, wherever you are—in less than one minute's time and for about one-third the price of a hardcover copy at Barnes and Noble. The question mark after the word "books" in the last sentence is to tease you about whether or not Amazon and the Kindle 2 have actually made both books and the term "books" obsolete. It may be more accurate to say that the Kindle 2 holds 1,500 expanded essays—or large units of text. (But, you might ask, without lots of books on my office/library shelves neatly arranged by topic, how can I silently impress and convince visitors that I'm a learned person?)

And Amazon didn't stop there, either. You may have noticed that Amazon has moved from selling books to being the world's largest online retailer of everything, not just books. And just in time, too—because as we write this, Google has announced that it's challenging Amazon by moving beyond searches of websites to providing content from books, so that when you "Google it," you're really going to be Googling everything!

Or quickly consider once again what Apple has done with the iPod, the iPhone, and iTunes. They've transformed the music industry much like Amazon transformed the book and Internet sales industries. With no CDs, no inventory, and a very small staff, Apple downloads specific songs directly to your computer or iPod for 99 cents or $1.29, all friction free—no one touches anything. Yes, CDs are "so retro" and going the way of the eight-track. And no, none of these giants of innovation stands still or is satisfied to be top dog of their market. They want everyone else's market, too, and have the technological savvy to go after it.

If you think that transformational technology is not being kind to traditional CD makers or bookstores, it's not being kind to newspapers, either. Why pay for a print newspaper and cause another tree to die when you can get your news for free from a number of sources on the Internet? Today's readers are going from hard print newspapers to Internet news, or, further still, to blogs. Wikipedia, the "for free" Internet encyclopedia, is quickly making Britannica obsolete. These examples are all about transformational technology, which is how TL2.0s think about using technology.

Cross-Industry Learning

And where do successful innovative ideas actually come from? The secret is that most industry- or profession-changing innovations are borrowed—borrowed from a different industry, business, or profession. A good label for this transfer of ideas is "cross-industry learning." Sounds better than borrowing or stealing, now, doesn't it?

What might the TL in education learn and do with what they see and experience through Amazon or Apple, or another business that customizes its products and services for you, while they also do it for everyone else? Here, for starters, are five steps that will put you in a position to do "cross-industry learning" and that just might help you transform education:

1. When a business, industry, or profession is customizing their services to everyone, ask yourself (or ask them), "How do they do that?"

2. Think about how their technology, their processes, might be used to customize services for students, parents, and/or staff.

3. Talk with your curriculum, instruction, and information technology people about the ideas that come to you.

4. Identify those ideas that have promise and make plans to implement pilot studies or other experiments to test them out.

5. Learn from the innovations that didn't work and share those that did work with everyone in your organization.

The Amazon and Apple stories are full of cross-industry learning that could move our schools from industrial age and mass production to the age of empowerment and mass customization. (Much more about how this applies to education in chapter 6 of *Learning Communities 2.0.*)

Experiencing the benefits of technology is great for the consumer. But if leaders are to understand technology to the point that they can apply it to their profession or industry, they must understand it at a deeper level. In the following shaded box are three excellent books for you to consider if you want to understand in more depth how Google, iTunes, Amazon, and other technology-driven companies do what they do. You don't have to be a techie to gain a lot from them—they're all written on a level understandable to the TL, and maybe even to the 80 percent leader (a bad attempt at humor here). These three authors tell you much more, of course, and when you are finished reading their books you'll definitely be on your way to being a cross-industry learner and leader. That is, you'll be ready to apply what other innovators are doing to how you can customize education and student learning.

Great Resources for Cross-Industry Learning

Everything Is Miscellaneous by David Weinberger. Weinberger will tell you how Flickr, Google, and Yahoo know what you are looking for before three clicks, and thereby tell you—the TL in education—how easy it would be for students to find the exact learning experience they need online.

The Long Tail by Chris Anderson. Anderson will tell you why you can get anything you want today, tell you how every niche is served, and thereby tell you how various online learning activities could accommodate learners' learning styles and interest levels.

Here Comes Everybody by Clay Shirky. Shirky will tell you how people can contribute to projects online, tell you how Wikipedia works, and thereby tell you how educators could create wiki-curricula and wiki-instruction packages for all students to use.

The Leader's Personnel and People Work

At the beginning, and in the end, organizations, businesses, and especially school systems are only as good (or make that "as great") as their people and their leaders. In possibly the most noted leadership book of the past ten years, Jim Collins in *Good to Great* clearly states what it takes to move a good organization to the next level. One of his memorable lines, and a line very relevant to educational leaders, is that level 5 leaders, leaders at Collins's highest level of leadership effectiveness,

> **get the right people on the bus, the wrong people off of the bus, and the right people in the right seats.**

Effective leaders would quickly and strongly agree with that statement. And said a bit differently: Effective leaders are very aware that they must be perceptive talent scouts, trusting empowerers, proactive retainers, and assertive out-counselors.

Attracting and Empowering Talent

Their goal: attracting, utilizing, and retaining talented, creative, and dependable people—the ones least likely to be standing in the unemployment lines in tough/tight financial times. As we've noted earlier, people with those qualities are not regarded simply as workers or employees. Rather, they're seen as organizational assets, as team members, as associates, as colleagues, and as any other name that denotes value and respect.

And these creative and talented people are fast becoming aware of their star status. With that comes expectations of their leaders and organizations—expectations that, in exchange for their unique productivity, they will be catered to. They will expect to set their work schedules and maybe even their work location and amenities. ("By the way, I will be bringing my dog to work with me.") But such tradeoffs are usually positive for everyone, since these talented and creative employees are the innovators and visionaries who create "wow" products and services that satisfy—even dazzle—customers. Yes, good/great people are hard to find and also hard to keep, and, as we noted in chapter 1, they have options and they're not afraid to use them.

In our transparent world, anyone (with just a little digging) can learn anything about an organization or a leader. Hence, attracting and contracting people doesn't begin with a job announcement. It begins long before that. Attracting talented and creative people today begins with your organization's image, its brand, its reputation. Being on the list of the one hundred best places to work gives organizations a great head start in attracting talent. And what your present employees say about you and your organization is also a strong attractor to would-be applicants.

As noted in chapter 1, empowerment works, and it's been working better and better as the technical and intellectual demands of information age jobs have risen. And as we'll make clear throughout this book, it's not a fad or just a fancy label. At heart, empowerment is about honoring people's uniqueness and deepest motivators. Empowering leaders both trust people and monitor performance. They both share their vision and offer people the flexibility to use their own strongest talents. They both reward people for their contributions and are candid about concerns.

By contrast, today's leadership literature shows that top-down managers who don't want to, or are unable to, empower people are likely to find themselves supervising workers who are not very motivated and not very engaged in their work. Yes, they'll do their work, but they'll also go home at 5 p.m., watch the Cubs lose a close one, and return to work the next morning expecting to be told what they should do that day and how they should do it.

Out-Counseling the Underperforming

Getting the wrong people off of the bus is the unpleasant part of Collins's three-part statement. It is easily the most difficult for educational leaders, since they tend to be caring, supportive, and positive people. In fact, many were hired specifically for those qualities. But out-counseling the marginal employee requires resolve and is critical to the success of teams and organizations. No, "out-counseling" isn't quite the same as "doing a Donald Trump" with a clear statement of "You're fired!" Yet the out-counseling leader must be clear that underperforming people cannot remain in their positions. Fair and caring leaders will sincerely work with them to help them find a position more suited to their particular attitudes, skills, and work ethic.

Happily, there are processes and skills—described in chapter 7 of *Learning Communities 2.0*—that make out-counseling the marginal employee less painful for both the supervisor and supervisee. If the candor, potential confrontations, and emotions inherent in out-counseling appear to be difficult for you, you may wish to learn about the process from someone who has been in that situation a few times and can share some do's and don'ts with you. The process requires good interpersonal skills, writing/documentation skills, knowledge of personnel laws and regulations, knowledge of your organization's policies, and the advice of an attorney with experience in personnel law.

Challenging the Inertia of Tenure

We can't leave the topic of people and personnel without discussing tenure. Tenure as a concept is outdated in today's world. In reality, it is far more often used to protect poor performers than truly outside-the-box ones. While it is controversial to take on this issue, courageous leaders must take a stand against poor performance and the inertia of convention and convenience, simply because tenure as widely practiced is so antithetical to organizational change and improvement. There are discouraging realities about tenure. One is that it is difficult to out-counsel/remove a poorly performing tenured employee. Another is more psychological, but equally powerful, namely: Very few leaders even consider removing a marginal employee—and, if the truth be known, some hide behind the myth of tenure so that they can avoid having to deal with the tensions and unpleasantness of the process.

When we think of tenure, we immediately think of teachers. But the same level of accountability must be applied to all levels and positions in school systems. Superintendents, principals, and other administrators who are marginal should also be out-counseled/removed. The bottom line here is that the education of children and young adults is critically important. School systems are not in the employment business; they are in the student-learning business. The acid test for TLs lies in the candid answers to these kinds of questions:

"Would I want that teacher to be my child's teacher?"
"If I were a teacher, would I want that principal to be my leader?"
    and ultimately,
"If I were a board member, would I want that person to be my
    superintendent?"

If the honest and thoughtful answers to these questions is no, the TL has the moral obligation to "get the wrong people off of the bus."

Besides Collins's *Good to Great*, the shaded box contains three more excellent reads on people and personnel.

Excellent Resources on People and Personnel

A Whole New Mind by Daniel Pink. Pink presents a strong case for how
    today's world requires that we use both sides of our brain—the left and
    the right are now seen as equally important.
The Flight of the Creative Class by Richard Florida. Florida helps us to
    understand the global competition for talent, especially creative talent.
The New American Workplace by James O'Toole and Edward Lawler.
    O'Toole and Lawler describe the trends and conditions of the chang-
    ing American workplace.

Character and Your Inside Work

Who you are is how you lead!

Translated, that means leadership development is ultimately personal development. Warren Bennis says it this way: "The point is not to become a leader. The point is to become yourself, to use yourself completely, all of your skills, gifts, and energies in order to make your vision manifest."

Delorese Ambrose says it like this: "Leadership begins and ends with the internal developmental struggles of the individual leader."

And Stephen Covey suggests, "We lead from the inside out" and "Leadership is an inside job." This is very much what we meant earlier in pointing out the central role that the inner dimension of EQ plays in effective leadership.

Core Values

Character counts! In the long term, character is more important to leaders than charisma and style. Trust makes everything work smoother and faster. Decisions can be made on a handshake; lawyers need not get involved; and we can get started on the project tomorrow, without endless paperwork and formal guarantees. Like many things that in the past were thought of as costly ways to do business, character, integrity, and trust have proven themselves to have a positive impact on the bottom line. What is morally right and fair is also best for the profit and loss statement. Behavior is quite sure to change when values and dollars are aligned.

A study of leadership literature of the past twenty years or so suggests that the following core values have near-universal approval. The list could have been much longer, of course, but we are listing the ten that we found were embraced most often. As you review and reflect on them, give thought to those that resonate particularly strongly with you—ones that are already a part of your personal and professional moral foundation. Identify the three or four that best define who you are, what you most value, and how you want to be known by your friends and colleagues. In other words, personalize each value and choose those that could have the largest positive impact on how you live your life and do your work. This is a significant part of your "inside work."

The list begins with the timeless values, those that we would all want to be part of our list, and then moves on to those that are becoming more relevant in the context of today's world. We provide a definition for each value. The definition may not be universally accurate, but it does reflect how the term is used when discussing Total Leadership.

- **Integrity**. The long-term expression and embodiment of honesty, fairness, trustworthiness, honor, and consistent adherence to high-level moral principles, especially those core values and professional principles recognized and endorsed by one's organization.

- **Courage**. The willingness of individuals and organizations to risk themselves despite the likelihood or perception of negative consequences, or fear of the unknown.

- **Honesty**. Being fully transparent, candid, and truthful, while being sensitive to the thoughts, needs, and feelings of others.

- **Reflection**. The process of using a values screen to review, assess, and judge decisions you and your organization have made or will make, and the actions you and your organization have taken or will take.

- **Commitment**. People's willingness to devote their full energies and talents to the successful completion of undertakings they have agreed to pursue, despite challenges and adverse conditions that may arise.

- **Productivity**. The optimal use of available time, resources, technologies, and talent to achieve desired results.

- **Teamwork**. Working collaboratively and cooperatively toward achieving a common recognized end, with individuals going out of their way to make the performance or results of others easier and better.

- **Openness**. Being grounded in a sense of psychological security. It reflects a willingness and desire to receive, consider, and act ethically on information, possibilities, and perspectives of all kinds.

- **Excellence**. A desire for and pursuit of the highest quality in any undertaking, process, product, or result.

- **Risk Taking**. Extending beyond the tried, true, and familiar to do different things a different way, often without the assurance of success. Risk taking involves taking initiative, innovating, and speaking out.

Principles of Professionalism

Principles of professionalism are those ethical standards of decision making and performance that transcend personal considerations and circumstantial pressures to promote the higher good of the organization and its clients. As with the core values listing, we begin with the tried and true, and then move to those that are becoming more relevant in the context of today's world.

- **Accountability**. Taking responsibility for the content and the process of decisions made, actions taken, and the resulting outcomes.

- **Improvement**. A commitment to continuously enhance the quality of personal and organizational performance, the processes used to generate results, and the results themselves.

- **Alignment**. The purposeful, direct matching of decisions, resources, and organizational structures with the organization's declared purpose, vision, and core values.

- **Inquiry**. The honest search for personal and organizational purpose, rich and broad perspectives on complex issues, and a deep understanding of ideas and possibilities.

- **Contribution**. Freely giving and investing one's attention, talent, and resources to enhance the quality and success of meaningful endeavors.

- **Clarity**. Embodied in the open, honest, and articulate communication of one's direction and priorities, the information needed for making sound decisions and taking positive action, and the expectations that surround work and personal relationships.

- **Win-Win**. A commitment to achieving and experiencing mutual benefit in the agreements people make, the relationships they establish, and the rewards they obtain from the contributions they make.

- **Future Focusing**. Conducting a thorough and consistent study of the shifts, trends, and future conditions that redefine a profession, industry, or organization, and taking a visionary and far-reaching view of emerging possibilities.

- **Inclusiveness**. Consistent commitment to maximizing both the range of opportunities for success available to organizational members, and the number of people included in relevant and meaningful organizational decisions.

- **Connection**. One's deep and genuine relationship with, and appreciation of, the value, intellectual, and feeling dimensions in oneself and others.

Identifying and Clarifying Your Personal Moral Foundation

Creating a personal moral foundation is a basic requirement for TLs. They consistently use that moral foundation as a decision screen and as a reflection screen in determining what's the right thing to do; and afterwards to determine if what they did was, in fact, the right thing to do. One's moral foundation can take a number of forms, but it typically includes:

- **A Personal Mission Statement**. A brief statement of not more than ten words that states why you are here on earth—your basic purpose in life. Here's an example: That people grow! It's a most appropriate mission for an educator and a mission aligned with our profession. And if your personal purpose/mission is not aligned with and fully embodied in your work, what then? Maybe it's time to update your resume and look for a position that is better aligned with, and more directly supports, your mission. Living your purpose is spiritually and emotionally essential to the TL.

- **Your Core Values and Principles**. Your core values and principles are compelling standards of what you believe to be right, fair, honorable, important, and worthy of consistent attention. They are the key criteria for your living in integrity. Examples

41

might be trustworthiness, achievement, learning. Identifying about five of them as most important to you allows you to focus on your moral core. If the number gets much larger, it tends to become a laundry list and is less helpful on a day-to-day basis.

- **A Personal Vision.** This is a clearly stated verbal picture of what you will be like when you are living, functioning, and performing at your ideal best—the more concrete and specific the better. You might want to develop both a personal vision statement and a leadership vision statement. To be powerful, vision statements should run well ahead of what you can now do—they describe what you're stretching to become. And they are more powerful if written in the present tense: "I am being/ doing that remarkable thing!"

These three components of your personal moral foundation should be viewed as a starting point for developing a strong moral compass for your life and career. It will certainly continue to develop and mature as you learn, grow, and gain more experience. But please keep in mind what Stephen Covey says about this: If things are important, they should be intentional! That means that having a personal moral foundation is only

---

Three Excellent Resources to Support Your Inside Work

Leadership: The Journey Inward by Delorese Ambrose. Ambrose talks about the effects that values and character have on leadership in a clear yet in-depth manner. This is one of the best reads regarding the moral foundation of the TL.

The Speed of Trust: The One Thing That Changes Everything by Stephen M. R. Covey. This Covey is son of the more famous Stephen Covey, and this is the best book we've read on the topic of trust. You'll exit his book with a firm conviction to become a trustworthy person.

True North: Discover Your Authentic Leadership by Bill George with Peter Sims. An up-to-date book that is a great complement to the authentic leadership domain of the *Total Leaders* framework—coming up in more detail in the next chapter.

going to work for you if you really pay attention to it, use it consistently, and allow it to strengthen and mature as you do. Alas, most people espouse having one, but few are intentional about creating, clarifying, and consistently applying it to how they live.

Effective Leaders as Everyday People

None of the people described by our leadership gurus are named Kent, work as reporters for their metropolitan newspaper, or duck into phone booths to change into their "Superleader" uniform when faced with challenges. Our gurus have been describing the real people who fill important leadership positions. And if we could accurately capture all of their ideas about the human side of these people in one composite picture, it might well look rather like this:

> Effective leaders are really quite normal people, very much like you and us. They have dreams, fears, children who are not always perfect and need to be driven to gymnastics, quite often go to church, feel insecure at times, and, well . . . somebody has to take out the garbage!

Before reading the list that follows, please stop and reflect on what our favorite gurus are saying here. And remember, Ken Robinson in his very good book *The Element* says that "How intelligent are you?" is the wrong question. The right question is "How are you intelligent?" Maybe effective leaders just happen to be a bit more "leadership intelligent" than some of us—since, for example, they

- Are mostly consistently good, honorable people, which is why they've been chosen to lead. You don't often get to the top of an organization by being mean and uncaring. Yes, there are some bad actors out there, and they get the press. But for every bad actor you hear about, there are hundreds going to work every day to make their organization and the world a better place.

- Are lifelong learners and always will be. How they learn is how they lead, and it's a permanent requirement of how they live life.

- Are focused not only on results and bottom lines, but equally on the development of the people they are leading. They know how to do both while enhancing both. Ken Blanchard's books repeatedly say that effective leaders are in the "people-growing" business.

- Demonstrate an almost paradoxical balance between being firm, bold, and courageous, *and* being thoughtful, caring, and sensitive. Yes, they've been known to cry when they discharge a poor performer. (Keep this one handy as you read the latter part of chapter 7.)

- Are values and principle driven . . . and they'd better be in this transparent world where your not-so-complimentary offhand remarks will be on YouTube tomorrow.

- Are not all charismatic and boastful. In fact, most are humble, caring, and optimistic.

- Don't usually shine in all the domains of leadership responsibility, but they know themselves and know their strengths. They lead through their strengths, while managing their weaker areas . . . frequently by selecting team members who are good at the things they don't do well themselves.

- Have a "life story." Their trip has been eventful, and they are good storytellers.

- Leave a legacy of the outstanding leaders they helped to develop, those that they made *Greater Than Yourself*—an excellent, recommended read by Steve Farber.

Yes, effective leaders don't leap tall buildings at a single bound or walk on water, but, just like you, they are very positive role models for everyone who comes into their sphere of influence.

CHAPTER FOUR
TOTAL LEADERS—THEN AND NOW

At the core of this book is the original Total Leaders framework. It's been an enormously rewarding experience over the past two decades to participate in and observe its evolution—from our earliest days of interest, exploration, and discovery about the essence and core of leadership and change to the blossoming of the TL2.0 version of the model today. Without question, one of the keys to our continued development of the model since *Total Leaders* was published in 1998 has been the encouraging response we've received to it from countless readers and users. And we want to highlight for you the two key things that stand out to us from all that feedback:

1. *TL* embodies a very comprehensive definition of leadership action that resonates strongly with readers' on-the-job challenges and experiences.

2. The TL framework provides solid placeholders for virtually all aspects of leadership theory, research, and practice.

For those of you new to this work, we believe that these two things in particular have led to the extensive use of the TL framework and book by a range of people and organizations, including

• Colleges and universities that offer master's and doctoral degrees in educational leadership

- Practicing leadership teams who've used it as a study guide, then applied it when dealing with leadership issues

- Job seekers who use it to frame answers to the leadership questions they're asked when interviewed

- Doctoral candidates who use it to frame their responses to the challenging questions posed in their oral exams

- Leaders and would-be leaders who use this comprehensive definition of leadership to guide their thinking, analyze their present knowledge and performance, and create their professional development plan

In short, we believe that *TL*'s continued popularity after being on the market for more than eleven years (without having been moved to the "bargain book" section) is due in large part to the practical realities it addresses and the validity of its key concepts and elements. But like all developments, there's always room for improvement, and that's been both our experience over the years, and the focus of this chapter.

TL: An Evolving Body of Significant Work

We regard the original *TL* book to be a snapshot in time—rather like the photos you see in family albums with everyone saying, "Wow, you sure looked less mature back then!" Well . . . true confessions: We became aware of that within weeks of sending in the manuscript to AASA for publication in late 1997, and the process of continued discovery about the model, its deeper grounding, and its arenas of application continues to this day. That's why this chapter is about the evolution of the model as we've experienced it, and we're sure that this evolution will continue as long as we remain open to the input we get from studying the work of the world's leading experts on the subject, and from our colleagues around the world who continue to apply these ideas to their work in business and education.

We feel there's something here for everyone—both those who are very familiar with the original *TL* book, and those of you being introduced to the TL and TL2.0 frameworks for the first time. For us, it's been a twenty-year journey of exploration and discovery, and every twist and turn in the road has been challenging, inspiring, and fulfilling. So welcome to that journey—and to the heart of our collaborative work!

In the Beginning . . .

For countless years we've joked with audiences that to steal the intellectual property of one person is called "plagiarism" . . . but to steal from everyone is called "research." Hence, we confess to being leadership "researchers" who are greatly indebted to the hundred or so gurus—our heroes and heroines—from whom we have been "borrowing" information and insights for years.

Studying the Leadership/Change Gurus

Yes, we are avid readers. And we're also lifelong learners, scholars, and synthesizers of all we read. That includes about fifty nonfiction books on leadership, change, the future, learning, and learning systems each year, and more than five hundred books and studies since *TL* was published.

The TL framework began to take form back in the mid-nineties, when we realized that no matter which new leadership book we picked up, its basic themes and findings sounded very familiar. That is, we'd come across them before in the work of someone else, but stated a bit differently and with a different emphasis. After encountering this a few times, we shifted our orientation from reading in order to expand our perspectives, to synthesizing the massive amount of information and ideas we had already gathered.

Analyzing What Leaders Do

Once this synthesis process began, we rather quickly realized that the leadership experts of the day actually agreed with each other on almost everything they described as effective leadership. But they didn't, and still don't, all focus on the same particulars. However, if we could observe them sitting around a "board of gurus" table, we're certain that each expert would be passionate about one or two aspects of leadership and state his or her case accordingly. But he or she would also probably be nodding in agreement when other gurus stated their particular cases as well. For example, Tom Peters would be nodding in agreement when Stephen Covey explained principle-centered leadership, and Covey would be nodding when Peters talked about vision and innovation.

At that time our list of the things effective leaders do included activities like clarifying the organization's mission, creating a vision, modeling core values, creating continuous improvement systems, creating feedback loops, attracting and selecting talent, creating a change-friendly culture, and so on—all things that our clients and colleagues readily accepted as key aspects of leadership. But after a lot of comparing and sorting, we discovered that these specific kinds of actions, which we now call "performance roles," began to cluster within five broad families of functional activities that we eventually labeled "leadership domains." Moreover, there were familiar labels in the literature that characterized these broad domains of action (i.e., authentic, visionary, cultural, quality, and service), and we used them to further our categorizing process.

Focusing on the Bases of Change

Once this happened, we began to see that particular clusters of *performance roles* and *leadership domains* were really essential in getting change to happen successfully—something that we'd been focused on throughout the previous decade. From our earliest days of collaborating in the mid-eighties, we'd become deeply aware that successful change required leaders to establish a series of conditions within their organizations that helped their people/constituents get past their natural fear of and resistance to change. Our experience suggested that there were four such conditions—which we initially called "bases," as in "bedrock" and "foundations"—and we diligently shared our insights about them with everyone we worked with. We named them vision, ownership, capacity, and support, and we could make a powerful case about why each one was a critical factor in the change process.

The good news was that three of the leadership domains matched up with three of the bases beautifully—one on one: cultural with ownership, quality with capacity, and service with support. What initially appeared to be "the bad news," however, got resolved fairly readily when we came to realize that our fourth condition/base of change—vision—was actually composed of two different things, purpose and vision. Once we separated them conceptually, we could see that each matched up perfectly with one of the other two leadership domains: purpose with authentic, and vision with visionary.

Getting All the Components to Integrate—Totally

In addition, the more we studied these five sets of connections, the more we realized that establishing these bases of change was a truly vital aspect of the leader's work because

**Without all five bases in place,
change efforts would invariably collapse!**

Once we began to think of change efforts in this way, we realized that an even better word for what we were dealing with was "pillars"—which hold things up and keep them from collapsing. Hence, the *TL* book calls these conditions the pillars of change, and it's why we've consistently stressed that *all five* must be firmly established and continuously addressed if an organization's leaders hope to get change to happen, and for it to stick. In fact, that realization is actually how we came to settle on the word "total" to describe the entire model—that is, a change effort must be "total" or it won't succeed, which requires the leadership input to that effort to be "total" as well.

A Deeper Look at Change and Its Pillars

A couple of pages ago we described ourselves as lifelong learners. Well, so are you. You can't be alive and functioning in Empowermentland without continuously encountering new things. And when they come into your experience, you rather quickly take lots of them into account and add them to the huge collection of things you already know about, are aware of, work with, and/or can do. To keep things simple, let's just say you're continuously learning and adapting. Bravo!

But don't let it go to your head—so are most people. They're learning things all the time, too, however small and seemingly inconsequential. And when you/they/we learn anything, our capacities expand. We grow, become more aware and capable, and something inside of us changes.

Our simple point here is that learning, change, growth, and evolution are continuous, natural, and beneficial human processes. They just happen as a part of us humans being alive and engaged in life. And so the only twist this book puts on this universal process is that, in today's age of empowerment, countless more of us are experiencing this expansion of our capabilities and opportunities, more often, and to a higher degree than ever before. In short, as humans we thrive on learning and change.

Addressing Education's Change Paradox

So this brings us to the paradox we've been addressing throughout our careers. If change is everywhere, and we're all doing it all the time, and our youngsters thrive on it, why do so many of us "freeze" when the word is mentioned—especially in relation to our place of employment? What is it that puts so many of us in "resistance mode" whenever the words "educational change" are mentioned?

We're not going to engage in a deep psychological analysis of that here, but we want to address it from the perspective that evolved for us as we forged the original TL model. We simply had to acknowledge that "fear of change" at some level or other existed for a lot of educators, and we were looking for tools/ways/strategies/processes that leaders could use to help their colleagues move toward a more future-focused, responsive, and effective way of creating significant learning experiences for their students. We knew that deep change was necessary, and we were quite certain that it wasn't going to happen without enlightened and decisive leadership—otherwise people would have already made the change on their own.

Furthermore, we knew, for starters, that threats of various kinds were not the answer. Whatever it was that leaders did to assist their constituents to acknowledge, embrace, and implement change had to involve way more "carrot" than "stick." And it had to take the form of an inspiring invitation to learn, grow, and evolve consistent with the times, rather than a directive to simply "Change!" and compliantly go through a different set of motions. In addition, we wanted educators to be operating at Maslow's self-actualizing level of functioning, not just stuck in the protective safety and security zones. And in every case we knew that these incentives had to be tangible and real for people—something they could see, feel, and touch.

Framing and Shaping the Five Pillars

So here are the five pillars, and we invite you to view them in two complementary ways. First, they certainly do establish the conditions that make empowering change possible. They give people an incentive to change and the psychological, technical, and tangible resources for doing so successfully. Second, they are really the ends—the "so what?" and outcomes—of leadership itself. Leaders don't just do a lot of interesting or inspiring things because they're . . . well, just interesting and inspiring. They do what they do to change and improve the "operating realities" of the groups/entities/organizations they work with. These pillars are the tools/resources they use for crafting those intended results.

Purpose

Purpose is the deep and compelling reason an entity/organization exists. It embodies the organization's ends, defines its intended results, establishes the "meaning" that activities have, and clarifies what it is ultimately there to accomplish. Without it, participants lack focus, direction, priorities, and "the reason" for doing anything. Confusion and lack of cohesion inevitably result. We believe that, to really be effective, an organizational purpose should be very brief, decisive, hard-hitting, and deeply motivating—something that people have at the tip of their tongues and really mean when they say it. If they have to look it up and read it from a sheet or poster on the wall, it's certainly not heartfelt or compelling. Here's one that meets all the above criteria, and more: "10:30." Sound familiar? It's from Federal Express, and boy, does it send a message!

Vision

Vision is a clear, detailed picture of what the organization will be doing when operating at its ideal best to accomplish its purpose. We've referred to it earlier as its "preferred future," but that's an understatement. It's not just preferred, it's ideal—the best possible job we could possibly be doing based on our highest aspirations and deepest motivations. Even though it's about things that far exceed your current capacity, you'll benefit from writing it in the present tense: "We're now doing this amazing thing . . ." And be detailed—the more specific and concrete the better. Why? Because your vision is your roadmap to success. It's your ideals, your aspirations, your job descriptions, your performance targets, your template for action, your effectiveness criteria, and your performance standards all wrapped into one. Holy moly! In short, it's your organization's total focus—your purpose translated concretely into who, what, where, when, and how.

Ownership

For us, ownership reflects the emotional and motivational investment personnel make to fully implementing the organization's vision and accomplishing its purpose. And it comes about in one key way: involving everyone in the purpose-defining and vision-framing processes. The more hands-on participation and involvement people have in shaping these two pillars, the more they will take pride in what's happening, see themselves in the results, and invest themselves in bringing those two ideals into action. Without their involvement, they'll lack the commitment to implement the changes implied in the purpose and vision ("too different"; "too much hard work"). And when the going gets tough, they're likely to hide, sit on their hands, or run for the exits. With it, they can clearly see where they fit in the change picture, what will be required of them, and why. Want a synonym? Try "empowerment."

Capacity

Capacity means having the knowledge, skills, abilities, and tools to get the job done well—with expertise, facility, and quality. And, once again, that job is fully implementing the organization's vision and accomplishing its purpose. This is the real "how-to" pillar in the change process, and it can't be shortchanged or overlooked because it represents people's ability to actually execute/do/implement what the compelling purpose and inspiring vision require. This usually requires a significant investment in building people's new knowledge and skills, and the more far-reaching the change process is, the more capacity building will need to be done . . . and over an extended period. Capacity building can't be handled with inspiring slogans and pep rallies simply because being high on enthusiasm is no substitute for being high on accuracy. People want to know they're "doing things right," and this is the pillar that guarantees it, or not.

Support

One way to look at the pillars of change is through the lens of being "support resources" for the change process—and all of them are exactly that. But in this fifth case, support refers to the direct, tangible assistance that the organization provides to its members to make the change happen successfully. That means organizing job responsibilities, schedules, time, compensation, physical arrangements, space, technologies, information flow, organizational structures, performance results, and technical assistance so that people can, in fact, (1) participate in the purpose-defining and vision-framing aspects of the change, and, in particular, (2) receive the capacity-building assistance they need to learn new things and improve their performance as the change unfolds. Without adequate support of this kind, people simply lack the opportunity to shape and make the change successfully.

The TL Model circa 1998

Except for chapter 1, the entire *Total Leaders* book is devoted to explaining the full model, its grounding in the literature of the day, and what it means for education leaders. With just a touch of embellishment, this is what the reader sees described there as the TL model: the integration of the five *leadership domains* with the five *pillars of change*, and the respective *performance roles* that underlie/constitute each domain. We've taken the liberty here of connecting the individual performance roles within each domain into a functional whole that changes the order in which they originally appeared in the *TL* book. This change better represents their integrated nature and gives the model an even more dynamic flavor. We've also replaced the name "cultural" with a better descriptor: "relational." So here's the model in "skeletal" form, with lots more elaboration of each element provided in chapters 5, 6, and 7:

Authentic leaders define a compelling organizational purpose by consistently

- Modeling the organization's core values and principles (which, combined with . . .)
- Being the lead learner and the lead teacher (directly support their . . .)
- Creating a compelling organizational mission/purpose

Organization members respond by saying, "The change has meaning for me!"

Visionary leaders frame a concrete vision of the change by consistently

- Employing a client/student focus (which, combined with . . .)
- Expanding their organization's options (directly support their . . .)
- Defining an ideal future for their organization

Organization members respond by saying, "Our new direction is clear and exciting!"

Relational leaders develop motivational ownership for the change by consistently

- Developing a change-friendly culture (and . . .)
- Involving everyone in productive change (as keys to . . .)
- Creating meaning for everyone

Organization members respond by saying, "I am a part of the change!"

Quality leaders build organizational capacity for successful change by consistently

- Developing and empowering everyone (and . . .)
- Creating and using feedback loops (as key resources in . . .)
- Improving organizational performance

Organization members respond by saying, "I can do the new things!"

Service leaders ensure support for successful change by consistently

- Rewarding positive contributions (and . . .)
- Restructuring to achieve results (as key elements in . . .)
- Managing the organization's vision

Organization members respond by saying, "Our leaders are helping us do it!"

TL's "Big Picture" Diagram

As our writing of the *TL* book neared completion, we found a way of capturing the essence of this full model in a diagram that actually expanded our understanding of the model itself. That diagram appears on page 122 of the book and a very slightly updated version of it is shown here as figure 4.1. It may take a moment to assimilate everything that's represented in it, but here from our perspective are the figure's "big picture" messages.

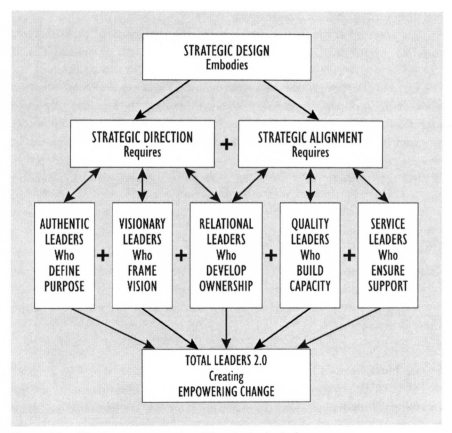

Figure 4.1. The key components of the strategic design process.

First, the entire macro process in which Total Leaders are engaged is called strategic design (SD). That's been the central focus of our work for more than two decades. Second, SD consists of two major components: strategic direction setting (shown on the left) and strategic alignment (and implementation) (shown on the right). Third, the key steps and elements in the strategic direction-setting process require the actions and input of three of the five leadership domains: authentic, visionary, and relational. (You'll find the whys, whats, and hows of this process explained later in chapters 5 and 6.) Fourth, the key steps and elements that make strategic alignment and implementation work also require the actions and input of three leadership domains: relational, quality, and service. This configuration of actions will be described in chapter 7 under the banner of implementing a "2.0" strategic alignment.

As you sort through the connections and dynamics of this diagram, note the importance of the relational domain to both processes. Yes, if change is to happen and stick, organization members must be kept involved in both strategic direction setting and in making that new direction really happen on the ground day to day. Also note the wisdom of an observation made to us about the diagram at the very first workshop where we used it in 1998: The role of school board members and the public in the overall SD process gets played out on the left, in strategic direction setting. From there on it's the staff's responsibility to get that direction implemented.

An Initial Set of New Understandings

From that point on, more and more things within the model, or how the model itself could be portrayed and used, jumped out at us, often stimulated by the unique issues raised by our audiences. Here are a few of the most important ones.

Seeing More in the Original TL Diagram

One of the ways the *TL* book portrayed the basic elements of the model was in a diagram that appeared on page 28. It's been updated here in figure 4.2—a part of the model's continuing evolution—again by replacing the original word "cultural" with the word "relational," which we

Visionary Leaders
Frame Vision

Service Leaders   Authentic Leaders   Relational Leaders
Ensure Support   Define Purpose   Develop Ownership

Quality Leaders
Build Capacity

Figure 4.2. The Total Leaders performance domains and pillars of change.

feel more accurately reflects that domain's essence. We're showing the model here because we want you to understand and begin to utilize some of its more fundamental theoretical features as well as its practical ones. Here are two of them.

First, note that when you focus on the pillars words in the vertical dimension of the diagram, you'll see words that represent the model's "production" features. The central component is purpose, linked to vision above and capacity below. In shorthand, this dimension is about identifying what the job is, describing what successful implementation should look like, and putting in place the personal skills and technical resources to get it done. Its basic nature is rational, technical, and achievement oriented— and, some would say, decidedly masculine. Then focus on the horizontal dimension, and you'll see that it's primarily like what empowerment is all about—mobilizing, supporting, and positively utilizing people to get the job done. It's also about inclusion, participation, and consideration for those in the organization, and has a much more embracing and feminine quality. In short, the vertical emphasizes "achievement goals," while the horizontal emphasizes "role engagement." Another way to view it is that one stresses ends and results, and the other means and processes.

These dimensions underlie very real tensions that occur within groups, organizations, and societies of all kinds, since they embody quite different sets of priorities and values. They also underlie a lot of what people think of as organizational culture and climate. The vertical stresses getting the job done—sometimes "no matter what." The horizontal focuses on the people asked to do the job and how they are being treated/managed/utilized. Neither one can be ignored; nor can it overwhelm the other without serious consequences to the organization.

So with this in mind, take a minute to reflect on these dimensions and how they play out in organizations you know about, including your own. Then ask yourself: What can a leader do to keep this dynamic "in balance" so that neither dimension overwhelms the other? Our answer is:

Be a Total Leader and strengthen *all five* pillars simultaneously!

The second key thing that has spurred the evolution of the model lies in identifying the basic nature of each domain. For *authentic* it's the inner character, openness, and integrity of the leader; you'll find that sort of thing represented in the center of other diagrams that we'll be showing. For *visionary* the premium is on imagination, flexibility, and innovation; that kind of thing will be located in the upper sector of other diagrams. For what we're now calling *relational* it's about direct personal connection, inclusion, and engagement; that sort of thing will appear in the right-hand sector. For *quality* it's about skills, performance, and improvement; its related elements will appear in the bottom sector. And for *service* it's about selflessly assuring that the organization fully supports its people; its related elements will appear in the left-hand sector.

Again, take a minute to reflect on each of these domains and the broad character of the thinking and action typified in each. Where do you see your greatest strengths?

Total Leaders—Total Professionals

Another key insight about the model's applicability emerged out of discussions concerning the principles of professionalism that we described near the end of chapter 3. These lively interchanges would inevitably lead to the question: "Well, what really identifies a true professional, anyway?" Over time a set of responses emerged that we could fit right on top of the structure of figure 4.2. Sketch it out as we've done many times, and ask yourself if this doesn't sound like the kind of "total professional" you'd like to hire—or have manage your finances.

Authentic = ethical . . . in their decisions and actions
Visionary = cutting edge . . . in their thinking and practice
Relational = collegial . . . in their work setting and relations with clients
Quality = expert . . . in their execution and assessments
Service = dedicated . . . to their clients and professional pursuits

Wow, would you like to have a "total" evaluation framework like this to use with your staff? Go ahead and borrow this one. Others have done it, and it's free!

Total Leaders—Total Decision Makers

Our clients have had some remarkable success using a decision-making framework built around five "I" words that reflect the essence of the five *leadership domains*: integrity, innovation, involvement, improvement, and implementation, respectively. In simple form, imagine a rather complex issue you or your organization faces. Then create five teams of people to help you "resolve the problem." Each team is given one of the "I" words as its primary criterion for coming up with a solution, and a given amount of time to do so. (For example, the "integrity" team knows that the decision/solution must align perfectly with the organization's core values, principles, and purpose.) Then each team reports back in an open forum with the other groups about its key criterion, its solution, how the two relate, and why this is the "best" alternative.

Two things usually result: (1) to everyone's amazement, each group comes up with the same solution; or (2) the group as a whole is rather quickly able to forge a "best" solution out of the five soundly reasoned alternatives. Why does this work so well? We think because the five criteria are themselves so sound and comprehensive, and because they evoke very "grounded" focused analyses. And, don't forget, you're free to simulate this process on your own. Just rigorously and creatively apply the five "I" words, and see what emerges that you hadn't considered before.

Zinger Phrases

For those of you who like to "cut to the chase" as leaders, have we got a deal for you (but only if you can remember ten words in groups of two)! Since we're both believers in the "less is more" principle, we've always looked for ways to capture the essence of the entire TL framework in the fewest words possible. Well, shortly after *TL* was published we achieved it—or at least a worthy contender for the honor. So if you can't readily remember all the complex stuff in our diagrams and frameworks, just think, and say, the following:

> For authentic—"Being real!"
> For visionary—"Looking beyond!"
> For relational—"Reaching out!"
> For quality—"Shaping up!"
> For service—"Hanging tough!"

But if these ten words are too much, we've got an ever shorter version coming up: five words that say it all . . . and more.

The Breakthrough to TL2.0

Up to this point we've been describing things that have enabled us to expand the utility of the original TL model, but here we pass the "tipping point" of our evolutionary process. What initially emerged for us late in 1998 was a realization that has taken our work farther/wider/deeper than we ever imagined when *TL* was written and published. And it came in the form of one of those two-word zingers we just saw.

The zinger was "Total Learners"! No, not Total Leaders—Total *Learners*! And it was followed almost instantly by the following realization:

**Of course! How can you be a Total Leader
if you're not a Total Learner first?**

And that one was almost instantly followed by:

**Because how you learn is how you lead . . . is how you live . . .
is how you learn . . . is how you lead.**

And for us a paradigm shift about the nature of the TL model had just happened, and the model had become at least three-dimensional, if not more. Moreover, as we said a few pages ago, "Total" means "Total," and this was about all aspects of life, not just leading. For the TL2.0, the nature of how you lead is a reflection of how you live and how you learn, and the connections among the three are inseparable:

Three Ls, joined at the hip, heart, head, and hands!

Actually, this new understanding of the model is what philosophers call "holistic"—everything is all a part of everything—completely integrated in all ways. When we said in chapter 3, "Who you are is how you lead," this is what we really meant. But now it has a much deeper ring.

A Search for the Model's "Wellsprings"

These first flashes of insight didn't instantly lead to a new version of the framework, but we instinctively knew that something deeper and more fundamental underlay the labels authentic, visionary, and so on. Thanks to the input of many insightful colleagues and lots more analysis, we finally came to an understanding of what we're now calling the *wellsprings* of the model. These are the vital sources of energy, intention, and substance out of which TL and—now especially—holistic TL2.0 with its "three Ls" flows. The wellsprings first appeared in print in Spady's *Beyond Counterfeit Reforms*, written in late 2000 and published in early 2001. But they've evolved further since then, thanks to more analysis and wonderful feedback from colleagues across the United States, Australia, Russia, and South Africa.

The Five Wellsprings That Underlie All Three TLs

As it happens, the five wellsprings/concepts we're about to examine all start with the letter "C." Hence, they've been called the "five Cs" by lots of people. But these five "C" words happen to be quite versatile, can take different forms, and directly support the model in various ways. Sometimes they're expressed as nouns—the names of things. Also as adjectives—the qualities and attributes that other nouns possess. Even as adverbs—the qualities that characterize actions—when people are, for example, leading, learning, and living. Moreover, we've learned that the adjective and adverb forms of the wellsprings can apply to an entire range of social entities, from individuals to teams to organizations to cultures to societies and even to civilizations.

So here they are, first expressed as nouns that "ground" the concepts themselves. These definitions were developed several years ago by members of the HeartLight Learning Community, an alternative high school in Port Elizabeth, South Africa.

- **Consciousness**. Our deep and full awareness of who we are and how we can respond to life in each moment.

- **Creativity**. Our intense curiosity to explore and express our rich imaginations and life's boundless possibilities.

- **Collaboration**. Our active participation with others in endeavors that enhance the standing and well-being of all.

- **Competence**. The willing application of our knowledge and skills to produce and achieve things of value.

- **Compassion**. Our deep sensitivity to our connection to all living things and our commitment to honor it.

And when we connect TL2.0's leadership domains with the energies and essences of these wellsprings, we can easily envision the following:

- Authentic leaders operating consciously, with intention and integrity

- Visionary leaders operating creatively, with inspiration and imagination

- Relational leaders operating collaboratively, with inclusion and involvement

- Quality leaders operating competently, with initiative and insight

- Service leaders operating compassionately, with intervention and influence

Next imagine applying the above definition for each wellspring to all three "L" words—for example, conscious leaders, conscious learners, and conscious living. Or how about collaborative leaders, collaborative learners, and collaborative living? Wow, the wellspring words almost say it better than the original *TL* labels do, and these connections begin to give an even deeper meaning to what we mean by both being a TL2.0 and the nature of empowerment! Yes, we're suggesting that truly empowered people would operate consciously, creatively, collaboratively, competently, and compassionately. And if they did, what an incredibly more harmonious world we'd have!

Finally, consider each wellspring word in adverb form, again connected to each of the "L" words . . . as in leading creatively, learning creatively, and living creatively; or leading compassionately, learning compassionately, and living compassionately. Or think about an individual, or a team, or an entire organization functioning competently, or creatively, or collaboratively. Wow, we'd sure like to be on their side at recess, or rooting for them in the NBA finals! Again, the wellsprings really portray everything we've discussed so far in this book in a new and richer light.

The Essence of the New TL2.0 Model

As you can now see, the essence and implications of the original TL model are far deeper and more expansive than we realized when the book came out in 1998. And capturing all those elements in one succinct diagram has proven to be close to impossible unless you consider a large matrix to be a "succinct diagram"—which we don't. We have however, created an expanded version of figure 4.1, which adds two key elements to the original model, and it's what you see in figure 4.3.

Those new elements are the five wellsprings that we've just been discussing, and the five definers of total professionalism, described earlier. Hence, when they're all included in defining the essence of each leadership domain, you can see how fully integrated and powerful each domain has become. For example, the figure shows that authentic leaders are conscious and ethical, and their key role is to define organizational purpose. Similarly, relational leaders are collaborative and collegial, and their key role is to develop constituent ownership for the unfolding change process. Take a moment to review and reflect on each of the five . . . and think about them applying to learning and living, as well as to leading.

VISIONARY
Creative & Cutting Edge
Vision

SERVICE
Compassionate
& Dedicated
Support

AUTHENTIC
Conscious
& Ethical
Purpose

RELATIONAL
Collaborative
& Collegial
Ownership

QUALITY
Competent & Expert
Capacity

Figure 4.3. The essence of the new Total Leaders 2.0 model.

But before we conclude this description of the new TL2.0 model, we'd like you to consider one more way the model has expanded. It's the TL2.0 as a "role performer"—in their organization and in life.

TL2.0s as Role Performers

In chapters 1 and 3 of *Learning Communities 2.0*, we'll be discussing a whole new way of looking at Empowermentland learners and learning. The concept, which we call "role performance" learning, has been a central component of our strategic design process almost from the beginning. Role performers are people who can competently carry out a complex range of related tasks across a range of situations and contexts. And we use a particular noun form to identify them—for example, producers, negotiators, and contributors.

As a bridge to that work, we'd like to share one version of how TL2.0s can be described in "role performer" language that also incorporates the wellsprings and pillars of change. These examples also come from a very advanced framework developed collaboratively with colleagues in Port Elizabeth, South Africa. So use them here to shape your own personal vision of yourself as a TL2.0. Just project yourself into the future with us and imagine yourself as

- An exemplary *authentic leader* in education—an aware, committed champion of learning—who consciously creates and sustains a compelling future-focused, learner-centered purpose for the change his or her school seeks to undertake that is fully understood and openly endorsed by all constituents.

- An exemplary *visionary leader* in education—an expansive, innovative thinker and opportunity creator—who creatively frames and continually refines an inspiring vision of the deep transformational change his or her learning community seeks to undertake that is understood and openly endorsed by all constituents.

- An exemplary *relational leader* in education—a receptive, collaborative communicator and team player—who collaboratively develops and sustains broad stakeholder participation in and ownership for the deep transformational change his or her learning community seeks to undertake that is understood and openly endorsed by all constituents.

- An exemplary *quality leader* in education—an adept, resourceful implementer and producer—who competently builds and strengthens his or her learning community's capacity for implementing the deep transformation it seeks to undertake.

- An exemplary *service leader* in education—a supportive, responsible decision maker and contributor—who compassionately provides and strengthens the support structures and opportunities that sustain the transformational change his or her learning community seeks to undertake.

While this may seem like a tall order right now, it will enable you to implement the essence of the TL2.0's mission:

**Shifting the paradigm of education from "schools in a box"
to "empowering learning communities."**

We'll be describing how you can do this in detail in *Learning Communities 2.0*. And besides, what could have more meaning or contribute more to the future of Empowermentland than this?

GEARING UP FOR YOUR
2.0 STRATEGIC DESIGN

Total Leaders 2.0: The Short Course

1. **Gear your organization's people up for strategic design (this chapter).**

2. Set a strategic direction for your organization (chapter 6).
   - Moral foundation
   - Mission/purpose
   - Learner outcomes
   - Vision

3. Align the total organization with that strategic direction (chapter 7).
   - People
   - Processes
   - Policies
   - Practices
   - Structures

All the rest is details!

The core feature of the Total Leaders model, whether in its original or 2.0 form, is its integrated approach to both leadership and change. As we said in chapter 3, they're joined at the hip: Leaders lead change, and lasting, productive change requires leadership that empowers. Like the old song says, "you can't have one without the other."

Therefore, the acid test of the TL model is whether it can bring about the kind and depth of change that you, the leader on the ground, are seeking. Clearly we believe it can, but that requires putting the model into action, and when that happens, all the separate parts that we described in the previous chapter get moving . . . and the whole picture gets a bit blurry. The nice, tidy categories laid out in figure 4.2 could be understood one at a time pretty much in isolation, but once in motion they lose their discrete identity. Suddenly the key elements overlap and logical sequences disappear, especially when it seems like many things need to (and almost do) happen simultaneously.

Yes, welcome to both the real world and to what we call the strategic design process—summarized in skeletal form above. It's what we think of as getting the kind of deep change you really want clearly defined, and then actually happening on the ground. The major components and elements of this process are shown in figure 4.1, and we're repeating them here as figure 5.1 to provide both a road map for where we are and a tried-and-true toolbox you can use to lead change in your organization.

The figure shows that the five major components of the TL2.0 model can at least theoretically be divided into two major arenas. The one called strategic direction (SD) enables leaders like you to put in place the key things that define and move their change efforts toward a new ideal. Those things primarily relate to your organization's purpose and vision. The second arena, called strategic alignment, enables you to put that new direction into actual practice . . . and keep it there over time.

And while we're not into intimidation, we sincerely believe that you aren't a real TL2.0 if you can't sketch out this framework in two minutes or less . . . appropriate lines and arrows included. Furthermore, as you gear up for the change adventure that lies ahead, we urge you to keep your visual of this framework (including the three performance roles that underlie each leadership domain) available and at the ready as you read, study, and reflect on these next three chapters. The visual will both remind you how all the moving parts fit together into one comprehensive, understandable, aligned, and doable process/model, and help keep you on track.

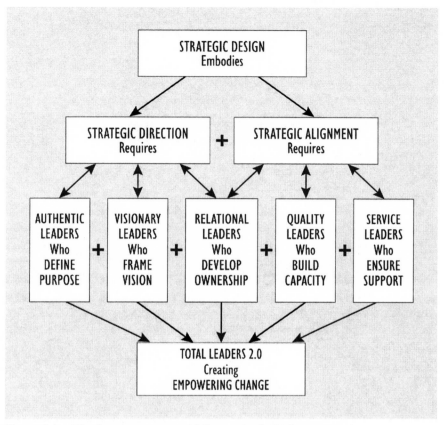

Figure 5.1. The key components of the strategic design process.

The Essence of Relational Leadership

The art of handling relationships well begins with authenticity: acting from one's genuine feelings. Once leaders have attuned to their own vision and values, steadied in the positive emotional range, and tuned into the emotions of the group, then relationship management skills let them interact in ways that catalyze resonance.

—Daniel Goleman

Seek first to understand, then to be understood.

—Stephen R. Covey

Profile of Relational Leaders

Learning, living, and leading collaboratively and collegially . . . enabled by a highly developed RQ (relational quotient)

The Gurus	Daniel Goleman and Jim Collins
Exemplars	John Wooden (legendary UCLA basketball coach) and Jimmy Wales (Wikipedia)
An Antithesis	Steve Jobs at Apple (creative and successful, but not a nice person to work for)
Mind-Set	We are in this as a team. Everyone has something to offer. We share everything—both the blame and the glory.
Purpose	To create a culture of collegiality, cooperation, innovation, quality, and success
Focus	• Human relations and participation • Creating project teams • Organizational culture
Change Belief	Change happens from the inside out when individuals are involved in, have ownership in, and are thereby committed to the change.
Performance Roles	• Developing a change-friendly culture • Involving everyone in productive change • Creating meaning for everyone
Key Sources	• *Social Intelligence* (Daniel Goleman, 2006) • *Integrity* (Stephen Carter, 1996) • *Here Comes Everybody* (Clay Shirky, 2008) • *The Seven Habits of Highly Effective People* (Stephen R. Covey, 1989) • *The Balanced Scorecard* (Robert Kaplan and David Norton, 1996)

• Relationships have always been an important part of leadership success; we just didn't know it.

As we noted briefly in chapter 4, the glue that holds the two mega-processes of strategic design together is the domain called "relational leadership." It's really the "people" part of the total process, and the key element in your "gearing up" work. Experience shows that without your people's willing involvement, the motivational energy and impetus necessary for making both strategic direction-setting and strategic alignment happen just won't be there. Great ideas and possibilities are one thing; motivation and persistence are another. That's why strategic design actually starts here—with relational leaders who build a culture and set of expectations within their organization that actively engages people and supports change.

One of the most frequently used descriptions of leadership that we've come across emphasizes that it's working with and through people to accomplish a goal. It's hard to argue with that, especially in Empowermentland. Yet what a contrast this is to some of the leadership heroes and heroines of yesteryear: George Patton, Vince Lombardi, Margaret Thatcher, Lee Iacocca, Jack Welch, Douglas MacArthur, and so on. They were far better known for their iron-fisted approach to motivating people than for their "working with or through people" relationship skills. They basically told their people what to do, how to do it, and when to do it. And they were very successful—back when authoritarian control passed for leadership.

But today's work world is different: Problems are more complex, and their solutions usually require a wide range of expertise, placing heavy demands on cooperation, teaming, collegiality, collaboration, and networking—which, in turn, require teams of creative and talented people. And as we saw in chapter 3, such people have many options . . . they don't have to "take it off of anybody." They want to be treated with dignity—even catered to—otherwise they'll move on. Personally, we think that relationship skills have always been an important part of leadership success (didn't Attila the Hun send his wife flowers from the battlefield?), but there's little doubt that they're even more critical to success in today's age of empowerment.

Goleman's Powerful Work

Daniel Goleman is our favorite relational leadership guru. In *Primal Leadership: Realizing the Power of Emotional Intelligence*, Goleman provides us with a framework for the management of self and relationships—the bedrock of relational leader success. For those of you with ready access to this book, turn to page 39 where he outlines "emotional intelligence domains." They fall into two parts: personal competence (how we manage ourselves) and social competence (how we manage relationships). Because relational leaders are aware of their own emotions, they're better able to control them. This is key to their ability to sense the emotions of others and build healthy and lasting relationships with them.

Goleman has three other books that should also be part of the relational leader's library—or in his or her Kindle 2: (1) *Emotional Intelligence*, (2) *Working with Emotional Intelligence*, and (3) *Social Intelligence*. All three demonstrate that there are many ways of being intelligent, and that EQ is more than twice as important to the success of the TL2.0 than what we conventionally call IQ. You may wish to read that last sentence over again, slowly. It is startling, and true—which is why anyone desiring to be an effective relational leader would be smart to use Goleman's work as the foundation for improving his or her self-management and relationship management skills.

Guaranteed, any work you do here would complement and support the work you did in the "Know Thyself" section of chapter 3—and we don't mean "once over lightly." For us, the first time through his framework gave us a cognitive understanding, the second time through provided an opportunity for deeper reflection and analysis, and by the third time through we were ready to use it for personal goal setting. You might consider that as well.

The Relational Leader's Core Attributes

Relationship building works better and faster for those who quite naturally trust others, who generally demonstrate trustworthiness themselves, and who enjoy meeting and working with others. RLs tend to trust people until they are presented with reasons not to trust. More cautious people tend not to trust others until they have shown themselves to be trustworthy. Since we tend to get what we expect, we're generally proven right, one way or the other. Chuck's dad had a saying that has stuck for more than fifty years: "Those who don't trust can't be trusted"; more often than not, it's proven itself true.

When facilitating problem-solving meetings, RLs expect everyone to have good ideas. Consequently they solicit opinions, ask people to expand on their initial statements, ask follow-up questions, and in effect, temporarily turn leadership over to the one with the expertise and passion on the subject . . . all the while building relationships and applying an effective problem-solving process. When making presentations, RLs give credit for accomplishments to others and to the team as a whole. When negotiating, RLs will seek and expect win-win agreements. When out-counseling an underperformer, RLs will work to find them other employment opportunities where they can be successful. Now, anyone can do these things in a manipulative manner, but RLs do them because they believe it's the right thing to do and because they come to work as the persons they really are: positive, relationship-building TL2.0s.

Moreover, RLs are basically nice people. You might recognize them by simply asking yourself, "Whom do I like being with at work? Who makes me feel like a contributor? Whom do I trust enough to be candid with about controversial issues?" And while RLs aren't all alike, they do have important things in common: They're humble, secure, candid, relatively ego-free, capable, courageous, honest, reflective, collaborative, and *productive*.

Relationships are dynamic and generally the source of meaning, joy, and success. But even healthy ones sometimes create conflict. As you might expect, RLs are skilled at interpersonal communications, problem solving, and conflict management. They are caring but also candid. They prefer catching people doing something right and rewarding them, rather than finding them doing something wrong and delivering a reprimand. They want people to like them, but not if it means ignoring poor performance. In short, the warm, accepting, and caring side of RLs should not lead people to assume that they will not be fast, confrontive, firm, and decisive when situations require it.

The Moral Foundation of Relational Leaders

Relational leaders are value- and principle-driven professionals. Were they not, trusting, meaningful, and productive relationships would be difficult to create and impossible to sustain. Their initiating side begins with core values, and their accountability side ends with those same core values—and not just when "all is well in River City." That moral foundation stresses the values of integrity and commitment and the principles of inclusiveness and win-win.

- **Integrity**. Valuing values. Relational leaders make decisions and take action consistent with a well-defined and widely shared set of values. Sometimes their value-based decisions aren't popular, but they don't hesitate making them.

- **Commitment**. Teaming, collaboration, and collegiality are commitment-building processes and structures. Relational leaders are the creators of commitment.

- **Inclusiveness**. Inclusiveness is a natural for relational leaders. Their belief in people demands shared decisions and shared accountability. "No one of us is smarter than all of us."

- **Win-Win**. Success is not a zero-sum game. "There must be a win-win solution hiding somewhere in this problem. Let's keep talking until we find it."

Relational Leaders Realize Fulfillment from

- Close, enjoyable, fun, productive, and lasting relationships that provide opportunities to reminisce and re-enjoy the past
- Winning as a team and embellishing that win with every retelling
- Mentoring the new talented kids who just signed on and helping them to be "greater than themselves"
- That letter of gratitude they occasionally receive that makes their day . . . maybe their month . . . maybe even their wall

The Critical Performance Roles of Relational Leaders

What we have described as the essence of relational leadership is embodied in three critical performance roles:

1. Developing an open, change-friendly culture (and . . .)

2. Involving everyone in productive change (as keys to . . .)

3. Creating meaning for everyone

Performance Role 1: Developing an Open, Change-Friendly Culture

> Whether or not leaders are perceptive enough to recognize it, organizations have cultures that take root, grow, evolve, and silently control the attitudes and behaviors of organizational members—even when, and perhaps especially when, no one pays them any special attention.

This quote about organizational cultures is a far more elegant way of stating something that we'd been sharing with audiences since long before *Total Leaders* was published in 1998: °

A culture embodies "the way we do things around here . . . when no one is looking!"

And, we might add, "the way we do things around here" represents a huge set of collective pressures that organizational members feel they need to conform to, either by actively participating or by silently condoning the words and actions of others. It embodies the "collective" paradigm thinking and moral foundation of the organization, as well as its "traffic control" and reward systems; that is, what it's perfectly acceptable to think, say, and do that will earn you the approval and even the admiration of your supervisors and peers.

Organizational culture is not only about what we called core values and principles of professionalism toward the end of chapter 3, it's about attitudes, expectations, assumptions, beliefs, and behaviors that define and shape everything about an organization's (or an individual's . . . or a leader's) character. Because the organization's character and its leader's character are mirrors of each other, this may be one of the most critical, yet often underplayed, performance roles in the entire Total Leaders framework.

The literature we've reviewed strongly suggests that successful relational leaders consistently embody and work to develop cultures that have two highly visible, mutually reinforcing features. First, the culture •

is empowering; it promotes personal initiative, improved performance, and organizational effectiveness. Second, the culture is change-friendly and openly encourages new ideas, dynamism, and lasting organizational health.

Four Things that Relational Leaders and Empowering Cultures Consistently Espouse, Embody, and Reward

- **Openness**. Grounded in a sense of psychological security, openness reflects a willingness and desire to receive, consider, and act ethically on information, possibilities, and perspectives of all kinds—including unconventional ones.
- **Innovation**. Employees risk trying promising new ideas, keep what works, and let go of what doesn't. Mistakes are opportunities for further learning, not conditions of "failure" or sources of blame.
- **Cooperation**. Employees pool their talents and cooperate in the workplace so that they can compete successfully in the marketplace. Teaming and helping others look good are encouraged and celebrated.
- **Success**. Employees recognize that it's the norm to plan well, work hard, work smart, keep learning, and win. When they don't win after doing their best, they collectively study how not to make the same mistakes again.

The four attributes shown in the shaded box directly reinforce what appear to be five dominant norms that relational leaders reinforce in open, empowering, change-friendly cultures. In gearing up to initiate a strategic design process for their organization, they

- Strongly focus on customers and clients because their needs and priorities change with the times. They keep their fingers on their pulse or risk losing them.

- Enthusiastically study the future, partly because it's fascinating and informative, and partly because their careers depend on it. They openly discuss the latest research, trends, and theories and how they can wisely apply them.

- Demand a flat, nimble organization by cutting down the decision-making layers in the organization and placing authority close to where the action is. This allows them to respond more rapidly and creatively to challenges that arise.

- Value risk taking and "good shot" failures. Because they focus so much on the best information around, they're willing to try things that show real promise. If those attempts don't work, they figure out why.

- Get creative people working together. They know that five smart people collaborating can tackle a problem better than one person can, since they feed off each other's insights and share the risks and rewards.

From our perspective, education leaders can benefit enormously from this emphasis on openness, collaboration, and innovation because the public schools are finally facing the kinds of market forces that have compelled business and other public institutions to become open, empowering, and change-friendly. Charter schools and home schooling represent major "growth industries" in the educational world because their advocates believe public education lacks the openness and change-friendly character that benefits *all* students. What an opportunity for relational leaders who recognize that change is here to stay and who are eager to create open, empowering, change-friendly cultures in their schools.

Performance Role 2: Involving Everyone in Productive Change

Whom should the TL2.0 involve in the change process? Anyone and everyone who will be impacted by the change—and from the earliest point possible. In the case of a school district, the list of "stakeholders" is extensive and definitely includes the students, their parents, their relatives, and their neighbors—any of whom might eventually be found discussing the change while selecting vegetables at the local Safeway. Do you want them to know what you are doing and why? Do you want them to support the change whenever the topic comes up? Well, yes, and yes. So if you are wondering if "they" should be involved, they should.

So why this heavy involvement in the change process? When we ask that question when working with leadership groups, the first answer we usually get is, "Well, if you want people committed to the change, you had better involve them in the change process." Hooray! It's a no-brainer, and everyone agrees! But if we wait just a bit and let the question hang in front of the group, someone will invariably suggest, "You might also get a good idea or two from the people who will have to understand and do the changing." Bravo; both responses are good reasons for widespread involvement. But which reason would the relational leader suggest first? And why? (Please stop here to consider your response before continuing.)

We think that the relational leader would involve people because he or she sincerely believes that they have much to offer, which emanates from the relational leader's number one value: integrity. Simply involving people just to get their buy-in can be viewed as manipulative and *not* acting with integrity—which, in turn, fosters suspicion and resentment. Integrity demands openness and honesty. Inclusiveness demands trust and high expectations of the participants.

For many, change is fearful and something to be avoided if possible because it is too frequently represented as "what those other people want us to do." In education, this is often called "fixing the teachers"—but leaving the rest of the system untouched. Relational leaders are able to avoid or modify this condition because of their ability to see change from the perspective of the staff and clients—as a process that happens from the inside out, starting with the paradigm perspectives, beliefs, values, and goals of the people affected. They know that when people begin to see things differently through new eyes and paradigms, and when they begin to feel psychologically safe, they can open up emotionally to explore meaningful change.

With a safe psychological place established, relational leaders are better able to recruit, include, and involve all of the organization's members and clients in the explorations that are a key part of the direction-setting process. This enables everyone to collectively define a purpose and frame a vision that give deeper meaning to the organization's endeavors and the roles people play that shape and support them.

But, as figure 5.1 shows, addressing these questions and involving everyone in the change process are not one-time events. For relational leaders, they're a way of doing business—a part of their leadership DNA. It begins at the gearing-up stage with developing an open, change-friendly culture, continues into the formal direction-setting process described in chapter 6, and continues on and on after that throughout the strategic alignment process described in chapter 7. So, TL2.0s continuously "think involvement, think asking significant questions, think getting good ideas, and think building ownership for the change."

And, if you'll allow us to mix metaphors, it's one of the five plates that TL2.0s have to keep spinning as long as they want to lead deep organizational change. Moreover, when those plates stay balanced on the sticks and the change happens right, somewhere along the way all those people will realize that they are not "making a change"; they "are" the change, and they "own" it. They are thinking differently, their expectations are different, they are functioning differently, and their work is more meaningful than ever.

MO of Relational Leaders

Relational leaders create a "safe place" for their people by helping them openly address questions about

- **Their psychological readiness for change**. How secure do I feel as a person and as a member of this organization? How does the change fit with my personal values? What's in it for me? Is the potential reward worth the obvious risk? Do I have the skills and abilities to change?
- **The organization's culture**. Are the heroes/heroines in this organization innovators and risk-takers? What happens around here to people who try new things and fail? Or who try new things and succeed? Are our leaders people we can trust?
- **The organization's structure**. What happened to the last major change effort this organization tried? Is the organization willing to change its structures and its way of doing business to accomplish its new purpose and vision? Can we trust our leaders to take the risks to significantly change the fundamental way we do things?

Performance Role 3: Creating Meaning for Everyone

Relational leaders are creators and promoters of meaning, and meaning emanates out of "belonging" and doing things of value. Here's where relational leaders in education have an enormous head start due to the profession's intrinsic value. If empowering children and young adults to lead happy and successful lives doesn't have meaning, then what does? If shaping and encouraging the world's next generation of leaders isn't valuable, then what is? Meaning is everywhere in education, and relational leaders never lose sight of it. Consequently they understand and continuously communicate that meaning comes from six key things:

1. **A compelling purpose**. We humans find meaning in doing work that is significant, makes a difference in the lives of others, and we personally feel passionate about. All work has purpose and meaning, but education work is top-drawer. Thoughtful and caring leaders identify and communicate that meaning whenever and however possible. Meaningful work leads to motivation, motivation leads to engagement, and engagement leads to excellence and productivity. Relational leaders never allow educating children to become "just another job."

2. **Seeing and being part of the big picture**. We humans find meaning in doing work that is part of something lasting and bigger than ourselves. Does the bricklayer think of his work as laying bricks, building walls, or constructing a cathedral? Each level of perception elevates the work's meaning and creates a corresponding level of motivation. We're betting that the bricklayer who's constructing cathedrals is more engaged in, committed to, and fulfilled in his work than his other two counterparts.

3. **Meeting challenges and high expectations**. Meaning comes from accomplishing challenging tasks and meeting high expectations. If work is routine that anyone can do, there's little significance or deeper meaning in it. This can be a key motivator for educators, and relational leaders know how to work with it. Challenge is everywhere in education, and parents and the public have high expectations for their highly diverse children. The rest you already understand.

4. **Being in control and responsible**. If being in control and responsible sounds like being empowered, it should. When someone else lays out our work and tells us how and when to do it, and we don't produce, we can easily dismiss the results as

"not our fault." But when we take on the responsibility to do the work and the leader puts us in control of the resources we need to do it, we take pride in our abilities, our accomplishments, and ourselves.

5. **Being part of a team**. For most of us, "winning" at something—doing it with excellence and flair—as an individual is fun. But "winning" as a team is multidimensional fun. When professional golfers win a tournament, there is jubilation for a moment or so, but the winners soon retreat back into their previous reserve and composure. They check and sign their score card and submit to the TV interviews with little emotion. But watch a close basketball game, and you'll see the winning team and their fans shouting, hugging, waving towels, and carrying on. Identifying with, and being part of, a recognizable team is emotionally energizing and meaningful. Relational leaders deliberately work to create teams and bring them together to win as a team.

6. **Feedback/keeping track**. Ken Blanchard is right when he says "feedback is the breakfast of champions." Without some form of keeping track or keeping score, how can anyone know how well they're doing? And without knowing how well they are doing, how can they work toward continuous improvement? Relational leaders create feedback loops that help people see how well they're doing. They know that keeping track creates meaning, that meaning enhances productivity, and that being productive in an important endeavor creates meaning. It's a perfect, non-vicious, empowering cycle.

Relational leaders believe that today's age of empowerment is a great time to be leading. They recognize that helping people find meaning in their work is the result of the culture in which they work and the involvement they have in shaping the direction and substance of that work. Both bring meaning to people's lives and directly benefit the organization as well. Education is full of opportunities for creating and experiencing meaning, and relational leaders really lay that groundwork as they gear up for launching and sustaining the strategic design process that's about to unfold. Welcome aboard!

SETTING YOUR
2.0 STRATEGIC DIRECTION

Total Leaders 2.0: The Short Course

1. Gear your organization's people up for strategic design (chapter 5).

2. **Set a strategic direction for your organization (this chapter).**
   - **Moral foundation**
   - **Mission/purpose**
   - **Learner outcomes**
   - **Vision**

3. Align the total organization with that strategic direction (chapter 7).
   - People
   - Processes
   - Policies
   - Practices
   - Structures

All the rest is details!

Setting a strategic direction for your organization is the most exciting and challenging aspect of being a true TL2.0. It gives you the opportunity of stepping away from decades—even centuries—of institutionalized, legalized, internalized, and reinforced educational thinking and practice; assimilating everything today's most insightful research tells you about learners, learning, and life; and using that fresh knowledge base to ask and answer three straightforward questions from an age of empowerment perspective:

1. Why do we exist as an organization? What are we ultimately here to do?

2. What kind of human beings do we want to send out the door, fully capable of thriving in the complex future they face?

3. What kind of learning system must we implement to ensure this result?

Then add "Why?" to each question, and you have it. All the rest is details! Well . . . almost, anyway.

Strategic Direction-Setting's Three Key Outcomes

Let's translate that for you. There are three tangible outcomes of the strategic direction-setting process that, in effect, provide your organization with a new grounding and direction for what it's there to do. The first is what we called in *Total Leaders* a "compelling purpose." It's a short, powerful statement that clearly defines why you exist and what you're there to accomplish, and it's your answer to the first question.

Your answer to the second question is perhaps the most pivotal step in the entire process because it embodies two key things: (1) what your purpose really "means" in outcome terms, and (2) your "ideal" picture/ vision for the learners in your organization. In our language, this second key outcome is a framework of life-performance learner outcomes, your tangible declaration of the results you're committed to accomplishing.

Your answer to the third question is your organizational "vision"— what you'll be doing and feeling when operating at your ideal best to accomplish your purpose . . . and the learner outcomes that embody it. It's the concrete, detailed description of what you're committed to putting, and keeping, in place to implement the new direction embodied in the previous two outcomes.

But there's more, and it's related to the additional "Why?" question we inserted after the main three. It can't be ignored, because answering it persuasively is going to be (politically) vital to the ultimate success of your strategic design. Every stakeholder/constituent in your system is going to want a sound, rational, appealing explanation/justification for why you're changing things, and why, in particular, you're changing them the way you are.

Elements of a Bulletproof Rationale

The outcomes of your change process require that you build a bulletproof rationale that contains four key essentials:

- A solid knowledge base of research, concepts, examples, possibilities, and sound reasoning that both underlies and bolsters each key outcome
- A clear and compelling explanation of the assumptions, beliefs, and paradigm thinking that both underlies and bolsters each key outcome
- A clearly articulated moral foundation—your core values and principles—that both underlies and bolsters each key outcome
- A clear and compelling explanation of the anticipated benefits that will emerge from implementing each key outcome

---

While the four essentials in the shaded box may seem like a lot of work—which certainly can't all be explained in detail in this book—this box represents the clearest and most succinct way we know how to describe it. And the good news is, most of these things result from the performance roles that authentic leaders and visionary leaders naturally carry out, which will be the prime focus of this chapter. So when we say, "All the rest is details," we mean it, with the following major caution.

Moving Beyond "Educentrism"

In this case it isn't "the devil" that's in the details—it's the assumptions, beliefs, biases, and paradigm thinking that we bring to bear on everything we do in life. We're human beings in a culture of a given kind that's embedded in a civilization of a given kind, and we've been through it and in its educational system for decades. In fact, most of us have been there for so long that we simply take most of its structures and practices for granted.

That's exactly where we were more than twenty years ago when we agreed to collaborate. We were educators, and both of us had doctorates—lots and lots of years being students in the system. Chuck was still a very successful, practicing superintendent of schools (how much higher in the system can you get?), and Bill was an international consultant committed to making the system he knew and respected way better than it was. As we explained early in chapter 4, we were both committed to educational change, but our work started out as "change in a box"—making the system we knew better than it was, but not changing its fundamental nature or functions. This limited, closed-system perspective is something we've come to call "educentrism," and it has placed almost impenetrable boundaries around educational thinking and practice for the past century.

We were constrained by those boundaries as well until we had a paradigm shift that, as Joel Barker says in his insightful video *The Business of Paradigms*, took us back to "zero." That is, we were compelled to reconsider, rethink, and redesign our whole approach to educational change. *Total Leaders*, the process we call strategic design, Bill's book *Beyond Counterfeit Reforms*, and this book are some of the key products of that shift, and boy, are we grateful for the experience. Why? Because it has opened our eyes to so many things about learners, learning, and life that just aren't on the educentric radar screen. And it's many of those very things that provide answers to that "Why?" question posed at the beginning of the chapter.

So we invite you to join us in exploring what authentic leaders and visionary leaders do to stimulate and guide similar paradigm shifts in their organizations—through the part of the larger strategic design process called strategic direction-setting.

Guidelines for Creating Your Vision

If you want to create a powerful vision for real change, be vigilant about these two guidelines:

1. Never ask an educentric question if you're seeking a non-educentric answer.
2. Never accept an educentric answer to a non-educentric question.

To assist you in sorting out the differences implied in the shaded box, we've developed a framework that we encourage you to use as you proceed with this chapter and as you undertake your own strategic design process later (see table 6.1). On the left is a range of educentric "mainstays"— things that have literally become part of the woodwork in education over the decades. There's nothing inherently wrong with them; they just bypass/ overlook/ignore a host of other rich possibilities. On the right is an empowerment alternative to each of them that we encourage you to consider as you broaden your perspective and shape your organizational Vision. This is the home base from which authentic and visionary leaders operate as they facilitate the strategic direction-setting.

Table 6.1.

FROM limiting educentric mainstays	TO expansive empowerment alternatives
In-the-box viewpoint	Outside-the-box viewpoint
Content-focused learning	Inner-focused learning
Disciplinary curriculum	Trans-disciplinary curriculum
Rational/logical thinking	Divergent/lateral thinking
Teacher-initiated/classroom-based learning	Learner-initiated/life experience learning
Graded structure and learning opportunities	Nongraded structure and learning opportunities
Academic achievement and advancement	Personal development and maturity
Transmission of accepted knowledge and understandings	Exploration of unique insights and possibilities
External expectations, control, and rewards	Internal motivation, control, and fulfillment
Premium on IQ learning	Focus on EQ development
Competitive organizational ethic	Collaborative organizational ethic
Quantitative measures of success	Qualitative measures of development
Closed-system thinking and operations	Open-system thinking and operations
Scheduled learning opportunities	Flexible learning opportunities
Getting right answers	Asking deeper questions
Adults as control and evaluation agents	Adults as learning and performance role models

In fact, as an ice-breaking activity when you launch your direction-setting process, see if your people can add to this list, even before the process officially starts. We think it speaks for itself as an eye-opening, perspective-expanding, paradigm-shifting tool; you'll want to keep it handy as strategic direction-setting proceeds.

Profile of Authentic Leaders

Learning, living, and leading consciously and ethically . . . enabled by a highly developed MQ (moral quotient)

The Gurus	Stephen Covey and Delorese Ambrose
Exemplars	Mahatma Gandhi and Mike Krzyzewski (Duke University basketball coach)
An Antithesis	Rod Blagojevich (disgraced ex-governor of Illinois)
Mind-Set	Who you are is how you lead. It is only when one has become an authentic, value- and principle-driven person that one is able to morally and effectively lead others.
Purpose	To establish a deep and compelling organizational purpose
Focus	• Personal values and life mission • Core organizational values and principles • Helping everyone to find meaning in his or her work
Change Belief	People will change when there is a compelling reason to change. I must articulate and model that reason to change.
Performance Roles	• Modeling the organization's core values and principles • Being the lead learner and the lead teacher • Creating a compelling organizational mission/purpose
Key Sources	• *The Speed of Trust* (Stephen M. R. Covey, 2008) • *Leadership: The Journey Inward* (Delorese Ambrose, 2003) • *The Eighth Habit* (Stephen R. Covey, 2004) • *A Sense of Urgency* (John Kotter, 2008) • *Credibility* (James Kouzes and Barry Posner, 1993, new edition 2003)

The Essence of Authentic Leadership

Who you are is how you lead.

There is no escaping.
Leadership development is ultimately personal development.

TL2.0 starts with and revolves around authentic leadership. Its moral and psychological character and influence pervade everything an organization does. Authentic leaders are masters of meaning and purpose. There is nothing pretentious or artificial about them. Their essence is value based and personally grounded. So you might expect that the authentic leadership domain gets personal—deeply personal. It should. Leadership is a personal experience. It is *not* a role one plays. Leaders are people, much like you and us . . . dreams, fears, and all.

The authenticity of the leader is at the heart of the TL2.0 framework. And while we chose to introduce the functional work of relational leaders first in this book, all of the other four leadership domains in the model revolve around it, are influenced by it, and are ultimately dependent upon it. Said differently, the purposeful way in which all five TL2.0 domains are carried out depends on the character and actions of leaders who are authentic in every sense of the word. When leadership is genuinely and humbly authentic, we may not even notice its presence. But when leaders lack authenticity, and that lack is exposed either by the routines of the day or by a crisis, trust is lost and everything about leading and managing becomes slow, cumbersome, and problematic. For us, trust is the WD-40 that makes possible a smooth, friction-free system able to maximize its resources for the real problems of the organization, and personal authenticity creates that trust.

Okay, all together now, in unison:

"Who you are is how you lead!"

In *The Speed of Trust*, Steven M. R. Covey makes financial genius Warren Buffett his exemplar for authenticity, trust, and success. Buffett, once the richest person in the world, lives in a small, old home in Omaha, drives an old GM car, and can seal billion-dollar deals with a handshake (no lawyers need be present) and things begin to happen on Monday. Buffett is authentic, his word is his bond, and his track record of honesty and integrity is a story. (Gee, is this the same Warren Buffett who donated more than twenty billion dollars to charity through the Bill and Melinda Gates Foundation a couple of years ago?)

The Moral Foundation of Authentic Leaders

Truly, who you are is how you lead, and authentic leaders embody and consistently model core values and principles of professionalism that shape and symbolize the moral character of their organization. So in this case, all core values and principles matter, but several stand out as essential to the credibility and unique influence of the authentic leader. To reinforce what we said about their key core values in chapter 3, they are as follows:

- **Integrity**. The long-term expression and embodiment of honesty, fairness, trustworthiness, honor, and consistent adherence to high-level moral principles, especially those core values and professional principles recognized and endorsed by one's organization.

- **Honesty**. Being fully transparent, candid, and truthful, while being sensitive to the thoughts, needs, and feelings of others.

- **Reflection**. The process of using a values screen to review, assess, and judge decisions you and your organization have made or will make, and the actions you and your organization have taken or will take.

- **Openness**. Being grounded in a sense of psychological security. It reflects a willingness and desire to receive, consider, and act ethically on information, possibilities, and perspectives of all kinds.

And the key principles of professionalism that serve as their standards for decision making and action are as follows:

- **Inquiry**. The honest search for personal and organizational purpose, rich and broad perspectives on complex issues, and a deep understanding of ideas and possibilities.

- **Contribution**. Freely giving and investing one's attention, talent, and resources to enhance the quality and success of meaningful endeavors.

- **Clarity**. Embodied in the open, honest, and articulate communication of one's direction and priorities, the information needed for making sound decisions and taking positive action, and the expectations that surround work and personal relationships.

- **Connection**. One's deep and genuine relationship with and appreciation of the value, intellectual, and feeling dimensions in oneself and others.

All of this, as you can appreciate, directly and positively contributes to the other key component of their success . . .

Knowing Yourself Consciously

Authenticity begins with "knowing thyself" in a deep and conscious way. That's why authentic leaders probe their inner selves beyond their commitment to their core values and principles of professionalism. They continuously go deeper. They're lifelong learners, and questions remain. For example, "What are my unexplored beliefs about people and goodness that cause me to value 'openness'? What are my unexplored assumptions about people that cause me to distrust some people and not others? Have I tested these beliefs and assumptions? Can I be objective about them? Can I defend them? If not, am I open to changing them, and ultimately my core values?" And, of course, when continuously reflective authentic leaders get most of this figured out, something happens to make them question their assumptions about their assumptions, and off they'll go to a deeper level of "knowing thyself."

So, in the spirit of the authentic leader's essence, please give this some serious consideration: Who are you? See if you can answer that most fundamental of questions by referring to the being deep inside you, not what you have, what you've done, the status you've achieved, the position you hold, or the "image" you present to the world. Just focus on the deep, inner essence of you.

If you haven't done much "inner work" before, you might begin the process by simply asking yourself, "Why do I do what I do? What causes me to think the way I do, talk the way I do, decide the way I do, act the way I do? What's down inside that's evoking these different responses?" Keep asking, and expect your answers to evolve over time as you become more aware of your inner self (as distinct from your public persona).

If you routinely make your inner work part of your total lifelong learning package, you may need only to consciously blend that knowledge of self with your role and actions as a leader. And please accept the fact that each of us is different. Hence, we'll each be beginning the journey of "knowing thyself" where it fits us and allows us to continue going deeper from there. Consciousness is indeed a journey, not a destination.

So, if you haven't done much inner work to this point, we recommend that you return to the last section in chapter 3 and revisit the "Your Inside Work" section. Completing the activities suggested there will give you a good start. Don't try to be quick about it. The essence of inner work isn't about writing. The writing comes only after deep thinking, reflecting, valuing, deciding, and committing. And if you really want to accelerate your process, we recommend revisiting the theme we called "the Oprah effect" near the end of chapter 1. Guaranteed, if you read any book you can locate by any of the authors listed there, you'll expand your horizons and your inner awareness.

How You'll Know Them

We've found the nature and essence of authentic leaders beautifully described in Cooper and Sawaf's book, *Executive EQ*. At their core, authentic leaders manifest high levels of

- Self-awareness of their feelings and actions

- Self-control of their feelings and gratification needs

- Sensitivity and empathy toward others

- Trustworthiness toward and in relationships

- Openness to new ideas and experiences

- Integrity to walk their talk and talk their walk

- Intuition that puts them in touch with their subconscious "flow"

- Resilience and adaptability in the face of disappointments

- Renewal and optimism when faced with the challenge of change

- Laughter and fun, especially when the going gets tough

In short, authentic leaders are those whom many seek out to be their best friend. They have their inner and interpersonal acts together as reflective, open, and honest human beings. But they're more than morally and psychologically healthy people. They lead by example and by establishing the most important thing in an organizational change process: its purpose—the absolute bedrock of everything related to organizational effectiveness and productivity.

The Critical Performance Roles of Authentic Leaders

Setting a strategic direction for your organization requires that you don two different hats, those of the authentic leader and the visionary leader. It may seem like an awkward task, but the natural overlap between the two domains makes it pretty easy. Both significantly contribute to creating the need for significant future-focused change. Authentic leaders do it by emphasizing "what's right" and "being real" about it. Visionary leaders do it by emphasizing "what's possible" and "looking beyond" the tried and true (no, make that the old and entrenched) for starting points and answers. Both are committed to paradigm change—no tinkering allowed! And both are convinced that moving school systems out of their bureaucratic, industrial age rut will take more than installing a new "block schedule" or a computer lab here and there.

Creating the need for change must bring with it a high sense of moral and emotional urgency. But public education's monopoly is only beginning to be significantly challenged, so the necessary sense of urgency for driving deep systemic change has been more difficult to create. Hence, that sense of urgency must be driven by three key things:

1. Acknowledging the critical importance of education to the future success of *all* learners

2. Facing the reality that hardly anyone other than educators themselves believes that our schools are doing an adequate job of preparing our students to meet the challenges they will face after they leave school

3. Highlighting the embarrassing gap between industrial age educentrism and empowerment age realities, as we did earlier in this chapter

Creating organizational purpose and creating this urgency to change is job one for authentic leaders, and they do it by applying their three critical performance roles directly to this direction-setting process. Those roles are

- Modeling the organization's core values and principles (which, combined with . . .)

- Being the lead learner and the lead teacher (directly supports their . . .)

- Creating a compelling organizational mission/purpose

And here's what each of them entails.

Performance Role 4: Modeling the Organization's Core Values and Principles

If creating a compelling purpose is the most important thing authentic leaders do to generate productive change, then articulating and modeling the organization's core values and principles of professionalism is the second most important. Why? Because authentic leadership, the central domain of TL2.0, comes down to credibility and trust.

With credibility and trust, leaders can mobilize and channel enormous reservoirs of hands-on, value-driven good will and loyalty, which is the engine that drives personal and organizational success. Without it, it's doubtful that they can get very far off the ground, let alone claim the title of leader. It's said that "leaders should turn around every now and then to see if anyone is actually following." Their credibility and trust, or the lack thereof, will be indicated by who's there when they turn around.

It is no accident, then, that we chose the term "authentic" to describe this domain. "Authentic" means genuine, real, heartfelt, honest, open, unadulterated, and trustworthy, and this is the performance role that most embodies those qualities and gives TL2.0s their moral foundation and moral compass. That's the "who you are is how you lead" part of the picture, and we can't overemphasize its importance.

But the other involves what authentic leaders must do to establish an explicit and agreed-upon moral foundation for their organization, and that's where the core values and principles of professionalism described near the end of chapter 3 come in. Get them out, put them in front of your people, explain and discuss each one explicitly, modify the definitions provided if necessary, and add to each list if it seems prudent to do so. But your critical step 1 in executing strategic direction-setting is to establish a focused and finite set of core values and principles of professionalism that your people enthusiastically agree to endorse, advocate, embody, defend, and enforce as the moral foundation of how you will operate from this point forward, period. No "yes, buts" and no excuses.

Will your people be able to say. . .?

"This is it! This is what integrity and professionalism mean for us. And we're committed to infusing them into every policy, procedure, and practice that we have."

Stop and take a deep breath. Now, please, we invite you to read the foregoing paragraph and shaded box again . . . slowly. Take your time and really digest it. This is the moral foundation on which your entire direction-setting process will rest. All three of your key direction-setting outcomes will be strongly influenced by what you publicly declare here. And once you declare them, then everyone in your organization can embrace and implement this performance role. In fact, they too will want to and they will be expected to model the organization's core values and principles.

How that looks, however, may vary a lot. Some modeling will be assertive and some gentle, some overt and some subtle, some emotional and some calm. It's not the style but the consistency that gives these behaviors their authenticity and credibility. For better or worse, anyone who chooses to lead is always on stage; not necessarily because they want to be there, but because we put them there. We watch them, we interpret them, and we judge them. The best

- Walk their talk and talk their walk

- Are up front and get going when the going gets tough

- Arrive first and leave last . . . and help put away the folding chairs

- Put up and pull through when challenged

- Honor their commitments . . . especially to those without power

- Stand by their word . . . even when that puts them at personal risk

- Give 100 percent all of the time . . . and a bit more when in a bind

- Bear the responsibility and give others the credit . . . use "we" and "us" more often than "I" and "me"

- Root for the underdog (natural Cubs fans)

- Ask of others only what they unfailingly demonstrate themselves

- Laugh when it's funny, cry when it is sad

- Are honest to the core

So this is why we placed authentic leadership and its three performance roles in the center of figure 4.2. It not only embodies the highly conscious moral foundation of the TL2.0 model and the core of the productive change process, it also directly influences the other four domains as well. In short, who the TL2.0 *is* defines what the TL2.0 can and will ultimately do, and that makes modeling core values and principles the centerpiece of any leader's profile of effectiveness.

Performance Role 5: Being the Lead Learner and the Lead Teacher

Authentic leaders lead the quest for continuous personal and organizational learning. For them, learning and being a lifelong learner are as natural as breathing. Even if they didn't have an organization to lead, they would be reading a book, listening to someone, trying new things, or simply observing some phenomenon to see what they could learn from the experience.

But lead learners *do* lead organizations, and they realize that in our rapidly changing world, continuous learning is required, not just of authentic leaders but of everyone in the organization, and of the organization as a whole. We agree with Peter Senge that effective organizations, especially those that are effective over time, *are/must be* learning organizations.

**More than simply adding knowledge,
meaningful and impactful learning**

- Clarifies or challenges one's values
- Challenges and even changes one's worldview/paradigm thinking
- Alters one's expectations
- Expands one's vision of the possible
- Ultimately changes how one thinks and acts

Authentic leaders are open to having new learnings impact them deeply, even when that learning is less than comforting. Guaranteed, this will be the case when authentic leaders commit themselves to establishing the knowledge base necessary for deriving the three direction-setting outcomes described at the beginning of this chapter: (1) a compelling purpose, (2) a framework of life-performance learner outcomes, and

(3) an inspiring organizational vision. And, as we will explain in more detail in chapters 1 and 3 of *Learning Communities 2.0*, that knowledge base had best contain some deep and insightful information about learners, learning, and life. Otherwise their change effort will be second-guessed left and right. With a non-educentric knowledge base such as this, they'll have a good chance of establishing both the necessity and credibility of the paradigm shift from educentrism to empowerment described near the beginning of this chapter. Without such a knowledge base, they can anticipate a host of arguments against making this kind of transformational change, and most of them will be based on "precedent." Oh, by the way, the educentric definition of precedent is "We've always done it this way before, and it seems to work pretty well for us."

And don't move on here until you've noticed that we've expanded the lead learner's role to that of lead teacher as well. First, lead learners/teachers have to learn and build their understanding/expertise/fluency with the essential elements of a non-educentric knowledge base. Then they have to be able to "teach"/explain/defend this new knowledge base to all their constituents. If they aren't fluent with it, they can't teach it; and if they can't teach it, their strategic direction will have a weak knowledge base. It's that basic, and that essential.

The good news here is that lead learners/teachers are intentional about creating learning organizations, and they don't leave anything this important to chance. They model self-directed lifelong learning and they openly share what they're learning with their people. You'll find them carrying around good books, showing off their new Kindle 2, talking about what they've most recently learned or heard, and encouraging others to attend growth-oriented seminars or to check out DVDs or websites they've enjoyed. Yes, they learn for both enjoyment and purpose, especially things that relate directly to ways of expanding learning opportunities for students and improving how their organization functions.

Moreover, lead learners/teachers encourage, expect, and support continuous learning by everyone in the organization. The question isn't "Did you read the latest issue of *Educational Leadership*?" it's "What did you think of the *Ed Leadership* article about the Illinois school district that has initiated what they call 'mass customized learning'?"

As you'll see throughout chapter 7, both lead learners and learning organizations are data driven. They gather, study, analyze, and learn from data about their organization—including its processes, products, production, and quality—and about other organizations as well. The focus is anything relevant to student learning or organizational effectiveness. And it's quickly shared with everyone who, in turn, is expected to assess its relevance to how they function and how they can improve. Learning organizations, therefore, quite naturally become innovative, "continuous improvement" organizations—with a far brighter future than some.

So, Are *You* a Lead Learner?

Here are some criteria for assessing your lead learner attitudes and behaviors.

- **Are you comfortable with being uncomfortable about what you know and don't know?** Lead learners reflect deeply, and they admit they don't know all the answers.
- **Are you a learning addict?** Lead learners can't help themselves. They learn even when they have no real need to learn. The true test is that learning doesn't stop with retirement.
- **Are you a good listener?** Do you ask questions . . . and then really listen, respond, check for clarification, thank the person for sharing, and (if it's true) tell that person that he or she just taught you something?
- **Are you hanging out with the bright and the bold**, the innovators, the good thinkers, maybe even with a "nerd" or two?
- **Are you forever young?** Can you talk with people much younger than yourself and be in the middle of the conversation . . . and admit your learning "takeaways"?
- **Are you excited about new technology?** Do you get the latest? Are you the proud owner of a 10+-pixel digital camera, an iPhone, *and* a Kindle 2? We live in a technological world, and to not embrace technology is to not embrace today's learning.

Performance Role 6: Creating a Compelling Purpose

All fifteen of the TL2.0's performance roles are important, but creating a compelling purpose heads the list. Not only is this performance role the most closely associated with the purest definition of leadership, it's also a prerequisite for the other fourteen, since an organization's compelling purpose drives virtually everything else it does. But if an organization lacks a compelling purpose, the other fourteen performance roles will lack direction and focus and be very difficult or impossible to implement successfully.

Our analysis of the leadership and change literature as well as our personal experiences indicate that effective, dynamic, and enduring organizations

- Have a clear and compelling purpose which they involve all stakeholders in creating, implementing, and maintaining

- Embody the values of the staff in defining that purpose

- Align all organizational functions and decisions with that purpose

When an organization has a compelling purpose, everyone knows where it and its people are headed. The purpose helps everyone determine what they should be doing, and equally important, tells them what they can stop doing.

As we noted in chapter 4, an organization's purpose statement (some equate it with being their "mission") should be very brief, hard-hitting, dynamic, and direction-setting. Our rule of thumb is: If it's over ten words, you've got an essay, not a purpose statement. The good ones we've seen in education usually contain the words "all students" and focus on equipping them for the complex future they face. However, the best one we've ever seen comes from Federal Express: "10:30." It's hard to be more compelling, dynamic, hard-hitting, direction-setting, and brief than that!

As we noted early in the chapter, four things will underlie your purpose statement: your knowledge base, your paradigm thinking, your moral foundation, and a statement of benefits. Let's just consider them to be your strategic direction's "rationale." The more explicit, detailed, and soundly reasoned these four rationale elements are, the more likely it is that your statement will withstand "the slings and arrows of outrageous fortune" that may come your way from diehard skeptics. So please get them firmly in place first.

Then note that your "real" purpose will take two forms. The first is the brief, hard-hitting statement we've been mentioning. Several examples appear in chapter 3 of *Learning Communities 2.0*. As you'll see there, this statement is more than a catchy phrase you can put on your school or district stationery, newsletters, or bumper stickers. They're the words that frame and shape your decision screen for what's important and honored, and what isn't appropriate or allowed, in your organization. The words you select are extremely important, but so is what you make of them. For example, if your purpose is "to enable *all* students to . . . ," then you should stop grading them on the bell curve. Words and their meanings are important to authentic leaders.

The second form your purpose will take is the framework of learner outcomes you'll be deriving as part of this direction-setting process. They transform your statement of intent into a tangible, dynamic, compelling expression of the results you're there to achieve. Many districts make this link by including a preamble to their learner outcomes framework that says, "We will know we are accomplishing our mission/purpose when all of our students leave our schools as . . ."—and then follows the wording of their outcomes framework. A brief example of what these outcomes might embody appeared in chapter 4, and a different one will follow later in this chapter.

The Case for a Compelling Purpose

In the absence of organizational purpose, leadership does not exist. And if the purpose is not compelling, why would anyone want to follow?

Profile of Visionary Leaders

Learning, living, and leading creatively with cutting-edge perspectives . . . enabled by a highly developed IQ (imagination quotient)

The Gurus	Warren Bennis and Tom Peters
Exemplars	Walt Disney and Jeff Bezos (Amazon.com CEO)
An Antithesis	The Bush presidents (each a moral, value-driven person, but neither seemed to get "the vision thing")
Mind-Set	Leadership is about future-focusing, thinking outside the box, vision creation, risk taking, and innovation.
Purpose	To create a bold and inspirational picture of an ideal future that will propel the organization into a position of sustained success
Focus	• Being a student of the future • Watching for opportunities for cross-industry learning • Encouraging innovation and expanding opportunities
Change Belief	People will change when they can see a concrete picture of an inspirational vision and when they know how they personally fit into and contribute to that picture.
Performance Roles	• Defining a preferred organizational future • Consistently employing a client focus • Expanding organizational options
Key Sources	• *Re-Imagine!* (Tom Peters, 2003, revised 2009) • *Seeing What's Next* (Clayton Christensen, Scott Anthony, and Erik Roth, 2004) • *Everything Is Miscellaneous* (David Weinberger, 2007) • *A Whole New Mind* (Daniel Pink, 2005) • *Competing for the Future* (Gary Hamel and C. K. Prahalad, 1994) • *Leaders: Strategies for Taking Charge* (Warren Bennis and Burt Nanus, 1985)

The Essence of Visionary Leadership

If your vision sounds like motherhood and apple pie and is somewhat embarrassing, you are on the right track.

—Peter Block

Visionary leadership is the future-focused, creative, imaginative domain of leadership.

—Burt Nanus

The essence of visionary leaders is paradigm-breaking imagination and innovation. For them, dreaming, creating, visioning, and innovating are the fun part of being a TL2.0. They excel at creating novel possibilities that others don't see; charting new directions and destinations for their organizations; and translating shifts and trends into productive options that transform their organizations. They look for creative options before declaring a preferred course of action, and they never routinely opt for the way things have always been done before. Vision is what brings excitement to the productive change process.

Authentic leaders are charged with clearly identifying the mission and purpose of the organization, while visionary leaders are charged with creating a concrete picture of what the organization will look like, feel like, and be like when operating at its ideal best to accomplish its purpose. We learned in the last section that people do not change unless they *see a reason to change.* Here we learn that people cannot change unless they can see a *concrete picture of the change*—and that's what visionary leaders are there to create. Organizational vision is the concrete picture and a manifestation of the organization successfully pursuing its purpose. It's what the organization will look like when it consistently and creatively acts on its moral foundation and meets its compelling purpose.

Visionary leaders are more than dreamers and unrealistic romantics, although both shine through a lot. They also have a pragmatic side that allows them to say,

This is the exciting place we need to go, here are the things we're going to have to learn to do to get there, these are some of the action steps we'll be taking as we get started, and this is what our Vision will mean to us when it's accomplished.

Because of their ability to look far beyond the givens in typical situations, visionary leaders are invaluable to organizations facing the challenge of continuous change and improvement.

The Purpose of Visionary Leaders

The purpose of visionary leaders in the change process is to orchestrate and lead their organization's vision-framing process. They use their skills to

- Involve their employees and other constituents in thoroughly investigating the challenges and opportunities facing their organization's future

- Develop potential scenarios and courses of action

- Translate those options into a clear and compelling vision of what their organization can and should become when addressing these future realities and functioning at its ideal best

The concrete, detailed, compelling document that emerges from this process is their organizational vision. This highly motivating statement demonstrates the quality and depth of the ideals that their change effort will embody when fully in place. With it, their ideal future comes to life in the present. Without it, the specifics of their declared purpose and intended change remain obscure, people hesitate to try anything new, and no one is ever quite sure where they stand as things unfold or unravel.

The Moral Foundation of Visionary Leaders

Like all effective leaders, visionary leaders operate from a clear moral foundation. When acting in their role of visionary, their most relevant foundation comprises the core values of openness and courage and the principles of professionalism of future focusing and clarity.

- **Openness.** What does the future hold? What are our options? What will serve our organization the best? This isn't a time for acting on bias or ego. It's a time for facing reality and acting in the best interest of the client, staff, and organization.

- **Courage**. The question can't be "What will I do?" The question is "What's the right and courageous thing to do?" Boldly laying one's self, reputation, and future all on the line is the visionary leader's way. Their motto: "Win some, lose some, learn a lot!"

- **Future Focusing**. Put quite simply, leadership is future-focused influence. Leading is a future-focused event. In a world of constant change, visionary leaders need to see around corners and over the horizon. (Remember from chapter 4, their "zinger phrase" is "Looking beyond!")

- **Clarity**. Fuzzy and/or differing expectations may be the number one cause of conflict between people in organizations. Visionary leaders honestly and openly articulate their motivations, directions, priorities, and expectations. No surprises!

The Critical Performance Roles of Visionary Leaders

Visionary leaders share with authentic leaders the challenge of creating urgency for change and the promise of change in their organizations. They do it by applying their three critical performance roles directly to this direction-setting process. Those roles are

- Consistently employing a client/student focus (which, combined with . . .)

- Expanding their organization's options (directly supports their . . .)

- Defining an ideal future for their organization

Here's the essence of each.

Performance Role 7: Consistently Employing a Client/Student Focus

In today's age of empowerment, the customer is king. The day is gone when companies and retailers were in charge. With a few clicks anyone can learn how other customers perceive a particular product or service, and the Internet allows the buyer and user to rate them. Their combined judgments can quickly make or break a product because customers believe other customers and they vote with their feet. Customers have many options in today's world, and if they have a choice, they often don't give underperforming organizations, or their products and services, a second chance. It's quickly off to ones that show more promise.

That's why visionary leaders in business repeatedly ask their customers, their colleagues, and themselves if they are meeting or exceeding their customers' present, emerging, and future needs. No, it's not enough to only meet the customer's present needs; anticipating emerging and future needs has, in fact, become the key to staying in business. Consequently, customers and the future are not "second thoughts"; they are the focus of all big decisions and actions of both visionary leaders and everyone else in the organization.

Now go back and read this same paragraph, but this time replace the word "customer(s)" with the words "students and their parents." Wow, does that send a message, or what!

The only difference is that the feedback systems about educational quality and results aren't as precise or sophisticated as the "product review" mechanisms available on the Internet, but they're getting closer. Today's reality is that parents have options regarding the education of their most prized possessions, and they are exercising those options more and more. Public schools once had a locked monopoly on education, but that monopoly is weakening. Education is moving toward being a competitive enterprise where the customer judges satisfaction and quality, which is precisely why home schooling and charter schools are the only things in education that are growing—except drop-out rates, of course. (Ouch!)

So how can visionary leaders in education best implement this critical performance role? Experience suggests four things. First, they can do the same kind of future focusing that their counterparts in business do—but instead of asking, "What does our organization face?" they can ask the equivalent of "What do our students face?" This, in fact, is one of the critical questions that are asked in the strategic direction-setting process that provides the knowledge base and rationale that help them derive learner outcomes. And it's exactly why we provided you with all the information in chapters 1 and 2; it's there to help you and your people answer this very question.

Second, they can add to this knowledge base irrefutable things about learner attributes, capacities, and "intelligences." We provide some powerful examples of these things in chapter 3 of *Learning Communities 2.0*, and we encourage you to study and use that material in conducting your direction-setting process.

Third, they can express their learner outcomes in "human" terms—in fact, in direct response to the second key question we asked at the very beginning of this chapter:

What kind of human beings do we want to send out the door, fully capable of thriving in the complex future they face?

We offered one example in chapter 4 of how this question was answered by a Colorado school district, but here's another—also just in skeletal form—from an Illinois school district that we've worked with over several years:

- Self-directed learners

- Self-actualizing persons

- Empowering friends

- Involved citizens

- Caring stewards

- Quality producers

- Enlightened contributors

Clearly, having learner outcomes such as these as your "bottom line" gives everything you do a client/student focus!

Performance Role 8: Expanding Their Organization's Options

If creating an exciting vision that propels the organization forward is the essence of the visionary leadership domain, then this performance role gives everyone in the organization permission to think as a visionary, to consider and formulate options that are truly outside the box, and to expand organizational perspectives and choices. Visionary leaders clearly let everyone know that they have permission to think outside the box, that they are expected to think outside the box, that they will be rewarded for thinking outside the box, that people will be listened to when they start their sentence with "What if we . . . " (You do remember those Hewlett-Packard commercials, don't you?)

Change comes in differing degrees. At one end of the continuum there is "cosmetic change," the "1" on a "1-to-10" scale. It's what we often call "tinkering" in our workshops. At the other end is "paradigmatic change," the "10" on the change continuum. In this day of mass customization, anyone who continues to think of schools as organized around classes, courses, class periods, and master schedules is at the "tinkering" end of the change continuum. If you are thinking like Apple does in the delivery of songs, or thinking like Amazon.com and the way they deliver books, and you apply that transformational technology to "mass customizing" education, you're on the "paradigmatic" end of the change continuum. Visionary leaders will love you . . . and you'll probably scare a conservative board member or two.

Joel Barker—the brilliant fellow who made "paradigm" a familiar part of our vocabulary—might say it this way:

Education needs a new paradigm. The old industrial age paradigm served us well during the industrial age, and we should honor that, but assembly-line instruction doesn't cut it in the age of empowerment and mass customization.

He'd probably also endorse the set of "from educentric to empowerment" paradigm shifts we presented early in this chapter. In fact, he might like them so much as an example of outside-the-box options for visionary leaders in education that he'd feature them in his next world-famous DVD.

Performance Role 9: Defining an Ideal Future for Their Organization

Here we are at the most exciting and significant part of the strategic direction-setting process, the place where visionary leaders consolidate and synthesize everything we've discussed so far in this chapter into their organization's vision of its ideal future. Although the leadership and change literature is somewhat inconsistent with its definitions of mission and vision, we believe that mission is a succinct statement of purpose, and vision is an idea, picture, or image of the future—a sense of what could be—in this case, in its most ideal state: the future state that the organization is committed to become.

Another way to say it is that vision is the mental picture of the ideal future of a person, team, department, organization, or world. It's the mental "video clip" that LeBron James plays in his mind when there is a time-out with the Cavaliers down by two with one second to go; that Nastia Liukin plays in those seconds of silence before she begins her floor routine; the tape that Steven Spielberg plays as he plans his next movie; the tape that Tom Rooney plays when he designs "mass customized learning" for the Lindsay school system. If vision creates focus (which it does), then concrete vision creates "clarity of focus." It focuses energy, motivation, actions, learning, and investment—which is why it typically spurs impressive results.

So, if you are not playing tapes about what your school could be, your team could be, and/or your school district could be, you're probably not in visionary leadership mode yet. To get there we recommend that you start dreaming . . . dreaming based on the intersection of (1) where the shifts and trends described in chapters 1 and 2 are taking our world; (2) the latest transformational technologies; and (3) what we know about learners, learning, and learning systems. Please think about this for a while—"what could be" when these three forces are combined in a vision about exciting learning opportunities for your students. And while you're considering this, keep in mind that

Visionary leaders make no small plans!

If a vision can be achieved at the time a leader creates it, then it probably should be labeled a goal rather than a vision. Powerful visions present significant challenges and run well ahead of the individual's or the organization's present capacity to achieve them. For example, NASA estimated that they knew about 15 percent of what they needed to know in order to get to the moon and back safely when President Kennedy communicated that bold vision for the U.S. space program eight years before it finally happened. NASA had eight years to catch up, and they did.

> **Useful, Powerful Visions**
>
> For a vision to be powerful, it has to be useful. Useful and powerful visions are
>
> - **Describable**, clear, concrete, and easily communicated
> - **Desirable**, representing an ideal future that excites and enthuses
> - **Doable**, but not without risking and heroic efforts
> - **Direction-setting** for both individuals and the organization

In addition to the four key criteria in the shaded box, a powerful vision must relate quite specifically to the things in the organization that really make a difference in terms of its effectiveness and ultimate success. One framework we've used with considerable success contains nine key elements, and "ideals" are created for each. They are

1. The student experience

2. The curriculum

3. The instructional delivery system

4. Student assessment

5. Technology

6. The staff

7. Leadership

8. Facilities

9. Community support

The following shaded box shows an example of element 3, the instructional delivery system, from a district we've been working with over several years as they periodically revisit and update their strategic design.

We've also developed an alternative set of categories that we'll be using as the organizing framework for our entire *Learning Communities 2.0* book—what we call an empowering learning community. It consists of

Our Instructional Vision at Skyport
How we help students learn

- Instruction and learning at Skyport are designed to meet the developmental level, the learning-style strength, and the interest area of each student. Students are motivated to learn at their individual maximum pace.
- Skyport offers a safe and secure environment for learning—physically, psychologically, and emotionally safe.
- Skyport makes maximum use of technology for learning. As learners advance in our system, more and more of our learner outcomes are mastered by individual students using computers to access challenging and exciting online learning. It is expected that high school students will learn 50 percent to 60 percent of their outcomes with technology, leaving teachers time to teach those most important learning outcomes that require a master teacher working with a group of learners.
- Because all curriculum is online, anyone can learn almost anything, from any place, at any time. Access to learning is 24/7 for Skyport learners.
- Most learning takes place in a real-life/authentic learning context where students are able to learn to deal with real-life situations. The community is truly the classroom. Learning and demonstrating learning through student projects is the norm at Skyport.
- Learning opportunities often do not follow a single traditional field of study. Most frequently, learners will be learning math, science, language arts, and social science while analyzing and solving real-life problems in today's world.

five key components that have strong parallels to all the elements we've discussed in this chapter and the TL2.0 framework itself (as shown in figure 4.3). Here they are in figure 6.1, portrayed in that diagrammatic form.

However, regardless of which framework you use (even your own), there's a paradox surrounding the framing of an organization's vision that you should consider. As Warren Bennis says, "Great paintings were not painted by a committee, and Visions seldom come from the herd." Yes, successful visions are usually the creation of one person, but they also require group commitment, ownership, and a broad consensus. So what do visionary leaders do in the face of this paradox? We suggest that they

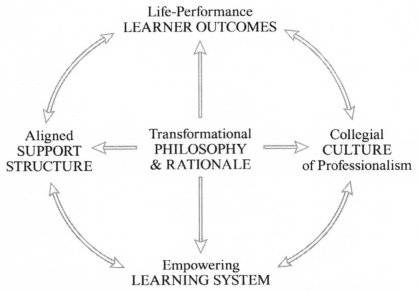

Figure 6.1. The key components of an empowering learning community.

- Put their own broad vision out there for people to consider, then translate into a final written product

- Show how their vision manifests employee values, core organizational values, and its declared purpose—that it's really in sync with what has meaning for them

- Encourage everyone in the organization to enhance, extend, develop, and personalize the vision for themselves; that is, write their own personal vision based on the organization's

- Always say "we" and "our," not "I" or "my" when discussing the vision

- Give (and give away) credit to all who've contributed to the final version

And here's a final thought to tuck away as you move forward into the strategic alignment part of this process. None of what we've described in this chapter would exist if visionary leaders weren't

- Seekers of the vision

- Consensus builders around the vision

- Communicators of the vision

- Clarifiers of the vision

- Models of the vision

- Keepers of the vision

Need we say more?

CHAPTER SEVEN
IMPLEMENTING YOUR
2.0 STRATEGIC ALIGNMENT

Total Leaders 2.0: The Short Course

1. Gear your organization's people up for strategic design (chapter 5).

2. Set a strategic direction for your organization (chapter 6).
   - Moral foundation
   - Mission/purpose
   - Learner outcomes
   - Vision

3. **Align the total organization with that strategic direction (this chapter).**
   - **People**
   - **Processes**
   - **Policies**
   - **Practices**
   - **Structures**

All the rest is details!

Setting a future-focused, inspirational direction for our organization is exciting. We get pumped for that. Motivation is natural and obvious when newsprint, markers, and bulleted PowerPoints are flying. When we finish our work, our spirits and expectations are high, and maybe even a few high fives can be heard. We want (or should want)

Profile of Quality Leaders

Learning, living, and leading competently and expertly . . . enabled by a highly developed AQ (applied quotient)

The Gurus	W. Edwards Deming and Jack Welch (retired General Electric CEO)
Exemplars	Steve Jobs (Apple CEO) and Katsuaki Watanabe (Toyota CEO)
An Antithesis	Chrysler (excellent with new designs, but near the bottom for quality)
Mind-Set	High-quality products and services are expected by everyone. Quality is an entrance requirement; continuous learning and improvement are the game. We need to do it better than anyone else.
Purpose	To establish policies, procedures, and practices that guarantee the continuous improvement of products and services.
Focus	• Customer/client needs, desires, and requirements • Continuous improvement of our people and processes • Empowering our people
Change Belief	Change happens when individuals and teams have the capacity to implement the organization's vision. We're here to help them develop that capacity.
Performance Roles	• Developing and empowering everyone • Creating and using feedback loops • Improving organizational performance
Key Sources	• *Good to Great* (Jim Collins, 2001) • *Greater Than Yourself* (Steve Farber, 2009) • *Human Sigma* (John Fleming and Jim Asplund, 2007) • *Now, Discover Your Strengths* (Marcus Buckingham and Donald Clifton, 2004) • *Strengths-Based Leadership* (Tom Rath and Barry Conchie, 2008) • *The Deming Management Method* (Mary Walton, 1986) • *The Circle of Innovation* (Tom Peters, 1997)

to tell the world about it. And, no doubt about it, it was work—but yet again, it really didn't seem like work.

For far too many leaders, however, just seeing that beautiful plan is enough. "Haven't we proven our intent? Haven't we shown our wisdom and creativity? Isn't our plan so right, so obvious, so inspirational that it will almost implement itself? We've all done our part; now it's time for the staff to get on with it."

This scenario is all too common in school systems, and there are all types of strategic plans lying on dusty shelves to prove it. For sure, meaningful change requires a reason to change and a clear vision of that change (see chapter 6), but meaningful and significant change also requires the capacity to change and strong organizational support for the change. If it's really going to happen, people have to be able to do it, and they'll need the total support of the organization if they're going to do it and make it stick. Yes, the heavy lifting part of being a TL2.0 comes *after* the strategic direction has been set—so, TL2.0, roll up your sleeves and requisition an NBA sweatband!

Good leaders are also good managers, and, as Marcus Buckingham pointed out (see chapter 3), they know the difference between the two complementary roles. While the lines aren't as clear-cut as this statement might indicate, leaders focus on values, mission, purpose, vision, and the future; managers focus on the capabilities of people, on managing the vision, on making things happen, and on moving the vision toward reality.

TL2.0s have two powerful leadership domains available to create the organizational capacity and alignment necessary to translate powerful new directions into the system's MO. The quality domain lies at the ready to develop and empower everyone and create the capacity to change, and the service domain is there to create new systems and structures that directly drive the new vision.

The Essence of Quality Leadership

You can measure quality but you can't manage quality. Quality is an output. You can only manage systems.

—W. Edwards Deming

When *Total Leaders* was published, bookstores were full of books on the topics of total quality management (TQM), continuous improvement, and Six Sigma quality. W. Edwards Deming, Mary Walton, and Philip Crosby were writing books, had their pictures on magazine covers, and were being quoted by everybody—including, of course, by us. Joel Barker in his famous video *The Business of Paradigms* boldly stated, "The quality paradigm is the most pervasive shift of the past twenty years." Where has all of that gone? Not much about TQM on the shelves these days. What happened?

Well, it hasn't gone away. It is now "assumed." Quality is table stakes, the ticket to the game. Once you are in the game you have to differentiate yourself with design, color, and/or hot deals. But if you don't begin with quality products or services today, there are probably large red-and-black signs in your windows announcing "Going Out-of-Business Sale." And to see how the quality paradigm relates to education, think of the fit Deming would have had if his son had come home with a B– in algebra! (Translated, this means that grades and quality assurance aren't compatible.)

Quality leadership is about developing organizational and staff capacity to change and improve. We learned in earlier chapters that people and organizations don't change unless there is a compelling reason to change (authentic leader domain), unless they have a clear picture of that change (visionary leader domain), and unless they are committed to making the change (relational leader domain). But even then, people and organizations cannot change unless they have the *capacity* to do so—the fourth of our pillars of change. Quality leaders have the orientation and abilities to stimulate employees to grow and develop as people and to establish ever-higher expectations and standards concerning the quality of their outputs/results and processes.

Deming was the most noted of all the quality gurus, and he believed strongly that the organization itself is the major part of any quality production problem. He demonstrated that workers could and would change if quality programs started at the top and leaders implemented the kinds of organizational processes that strengthen and support workers' abilities. Originally Deming claimed that around 85 percent of the functional and quality problems in any organization are caused by the organization itself, and only about 15 percent are caused by the workers. Later in his career, he changed those figures to 94 and 6 percent respectively.

What a lesson this is for education! Educators are members of the world's most important profession and operate a people-intensive business. Surely student learning success deserves at least as much quality emphasis as does a Lexus!

Four Keys to Quality Assurance

There are four basic aspects of quality assurance that form a continuous cycle:

1. Understanding customer/client needs

2. Setting quality standards

3. Measuring product quality

4. Modifying the process to ensure improved results

Quality leaders, of course, do them all, and do them all continuously and systematically.

To bring home the power of this cycle to education, consider the impact that not identifying learner needs, or not setting quality standards, and/or not measuring learner outcomes would have on the "modifying the process" aspect of continuous improvement. Without any one of them, decision makers could assume that there was no need for change, blame the learners for poor learning results, and/or take shots in the dark at improvement. In the end, these four aspects of the continuous improvement cycle embody a very logical process, are easy to understand, and are easy to support. Implementing the process is of course a bit more complex, but quality leaders embrace the opportunity and challenge.

Four Keys to Quality Professional Development

There are also four major aspects to the professional development process that reflect the critical pillars of change that underlie everything embodied in the TL2.0 model:

- All participants must be given an opportunity to acquire the knowledge and skills needed to shape and fully understand the organization's declared purpose and vision (the authentic and visionary leadership domains).

- By participating actively in shaping the organization's purpose and vision from the ground up, participants have ownership for them (the relational leadership domain).

- Development focuses on the capacity to execute the vision. Otherwise, it will be an empty promise that offers opportunities and delegates responsibilities, but participants will lack the skills and tools to implement it successfully (the quality leadership domain).

- Development depends on organizational support—the determination by those in authority to make the decisions, create the opportunities, devote the time and resources, and coordinate participants' efforts as they build the purpose, vision, ownership, and capacity necessary for successful planning and implementation (the service leadership domain).

The Moral Foundation of Quality Leaders

Our reading and synthesis of the leadership and change literature strongly suggests that quality leaders openly endorse, consistently model, and clearly exemplify the core values of excellence and productivity, and the professional principles of accountability and improvement.

- **Excellence**. For quality leaders, excellence and quality are synonyms. By this standard, if your work is not what you would label and judge as your best, you haven't finished yet.

- **Productivity**. We want to get things done as well as enjoy doing them. Quality leaders value accomplishment, achievement, and getting things done—well and on time!

- **Accountability**. Quality leaders openly and comfortably take responsibility for themselves and for their team. They volunteer rather than duck, and solve problems rather than place blame.

- **Improvement**. Quality leaders know and accept that quality is transitory and an ever-moving target. Today's "outstanding" will become tomorrow's "good" and end up in the bargain bin unless steps are taken to improve it.

The Critical Performance Roles of Quality Leaders

Quality leadership is shaped through consistent attention to three critical performance roles, each of which helps drive organizational alignment:

- Developing and empowering everyone (and . . .)

- Creating and using feedback loops (as key resources in . . .)

- Improving organizational performance

Here's what they look like in action.

Performance Role 10: Developing and Empowering Everyone

Developing and empowering everyone is the quality leader's most critical performance role, and it contains a unique challenge. If beauty is in the eye of the beholder, then the psychological condition called "empowerment" resides in the perceptions and feelings of the empowered. If the "empowerees" don't feel empowered, then they aren't, and they won't behave that way—no matter what leaders may say or do. To us, empowerment is

**Being in control of the variables that you perceive
to be important to "your" success.**

Leaders can do their best to establish conditions that maximize personal control of those important variables, but they can't guarantee that their people will respond accordingly. Empowering people works well under two key conditions: (1) when the empowered understand and are committed to the purpose/mission and vision of the organization, and (2) when they are mature enough to

- Set high, yet attainable, goals for themselves

- Take responsibility for performing the role they are in

- Be willing to take responsibility for their feelings, decisions, and actions

- Receive constructive feedback and coaching

In cases where these conditions are lacking, quality leaders have the option of putting on their "out-counseling hats"—something we'll be explaining more in this chapter and in chapter 7 of *Learning Communities 2.0*.

Otherwise, you can rest assured that quality leaders are intentional about empowering people and don't leave empowerment to chance. You can count on them to be proactive and take the initiative by

- Explaining and defining empowerment to everyone

- Saying they want it and expect it

- Making it an organizational value and norm

- Setting ambitious, vision-based goals

- Determining the maturity levels of personnel and assessing their readiness to meet the four criteria just listed

- Observing, monitoring, and coaching

- Providing the technical training needed for success

- Rewarding and celebrating the successes of those who are empowered

- Helping the empowered create bold, new visions of the possible

Continuous Learning

Before "change" became "rapid change" became "continuous change," staff development was generally thought to be the responsibility of the organization. Rapid and continuous change brought the expectation that all staff need to be self-directed, lifelong learners—largely responsible for keeping themselves up-to-date and employable. For quality leaders this means adding "continuous learning and development" as a critical feature of the organization's open, change-friendly culture as described in chapter 5. This and empowering people to maximize their individual talents are both "job one." Both are powerful leverage points for developing the organization's capacity to implement its strategic direction successfully.

But in today's shrunken world, learning has to be "global," not just "technical." Being a lifelong learner in our age of empowerment takes us beyond our borders and our profession. We need to become both generalist learners and global decision makers—things that clearly overlap with the outside-the-box orientations of visionary leaders—while staying focused on what it takes to acquire the capacity to realize our new purpose and vision. Here quality leaders, with heavy-duty participation of the staff, identify those skills most economically learned in groups and plan workshops and seminars for that purpose. Moreover, they help individuals identify their specific learning needs and provide encouragement, incentives, and support for individual/personalized learning.

If Joel Barker is right about everyone going back to zero when a paradigm shifts, the need to learn new skills, new approaches, and new processes becomes imperative when organizations set strategic directions that demand experimentation, innovation, and risk taking into new arenas of endeavor—something very likely to happen to education when it truly becomes future focused and learner centered.

Performance Role 11: Creating and Using Feedback Loops

Leadership guru Ken Blanchard says that feedback is "the breakfast of champions," but we have yet to see W. Edwards Deming's likeness on the front of a Wheaties box. Maybe we should, because Blanchard is right on, and there is no larger mythical champion for feedback loops and continuous improvement than Deming. In short, feedback is the process that helps us determine the impact of our actions. It provides us with the information we need to determine if and how we should change the way we are doing things in order to improve both our processes and our results. Try as we might, it's hard to think of a situation where we can systematically and continuously improve our performance without having some type of feedback to guide us—even if self-generated.

When thinking of quality leaders, it's easy to conjure up pictures of people with green-billed caps poring over statistics, as we might imagine Deming doing with his colleagues from Toyota decades ago. And sometimes, that *is* how they do things. But some of the most important and critical feedback we receive is about the more subjective and qualitative aspects of quality, continuous improvement, and growth. Every life experience gives us feedback—some from others, some intended, and some unintended.

But quality leaders are intentional about feedback, both when giving it and when asking for it. They know what they want to measure and improve, they design feedback loops that will provide them with the data they seek, they gather and analyze it, and they make decisions and changes based on their analyses. They also expect everyone in the organization to create feedback loops and establish continuous improvement expectations for themselves as well. That's how recipes get tweaked based on taste, golf swings get altered based on that last errant shot, and "pickup lines" get refined based on refusals or near misses. Those unaware of feedback loops continue making cookies that are not sweet enough, hitting shots that go too far right, and spending many evenings alone.

Creating Feedback Loops

Creating a feedback loop is a very logical but somewhat complex process. Whether producing widgets or educating children, there are six steps to designing and implementing a sound feedback process. School systems that have clearly defined their student outcomes and performance standards, and have built a system for authentically assessing them, will have a head start in creating feedback loops that are objective, meaningful, and growth producing. Here are the six steps that really matter:

1. **Clearly identify the product/service**. While some educators might struggle to identify their product, the verdict is already in: It's *student learning*. When educators have clearly defined student outcomes (as we describe in detail in chapter 4 of *Learning Communities 2.0*), the product is students' demonstrations of those outcomes.

2. **Set quality standards with a heavy-duty focus on customers and clients**. For educators, quality standards often come in the form of rubrics that help practitioners determine the degree to which students' demonstrations of learning meet predetermined high-level performance criteria.

3. **Identify the data needed to measure quality standards**. For teachers, these data may be the number or percentage of students who are demonstrating particular outcomes at a given level of proficiency. Teachers will need to specify which students are able to do which things at which levels.

4. **Determine how to collect, analyze, and communicate those data to all decision makers**. This step requires decisions about where and how students will be assessed, how the performance data will be compiled, what form the report will take, who is to receive the data, and when to expect that the data will be available for review, study, and analysis.

5. **Establish a process to ensure that the data are being used effectively**. Just because people are receiving student performance data doesn't mean they are using it, or using it effectively. If the feedback received isn't used for making focused improvement decisions, then the previous steps have been a waste of time.

6. **Continuously improve the effectiveness of the process of production and the effectiveness of the feedback loop**. This step is why one does the previous five steps, and it's the focus of performance role 12.

Quality leaders know that feedback loops are the backbone of continuous improvement. What Deming and his colleagues taught the Japanese about quality and feedback after World War II is as necessary in schools today as it is at Toyota or Nordstrom. (Note: For all its limitations and faults, the No Child Left Behind initiative has made educators more aware of the need for feedback loops and the skills necessary to implement them than any other "reform" strategy educators have ever tried.) So let's try this comparison on for size.

We are writing this book in the midst of the economic crisis of 2008–2009, and the government's intervention in the Chrysler company has been in the headlines. Chrysler has a reputation for building vehicles that, when compared with overseas competitors, are lower-quality gas-guzzlers, and it has enough feedback loops to recognize, if not accept, that fact—*Consumer Reports* and owner satisfaction data being two big ones.

So, if Chrysler were a school system, it could solve this problem by putting a grade on each vehicle as it came off the assembly line. For example, trucks with almost no defects would have no lemons on the window sticker; those meeting 94 percent of their quality standards would get one lemon; those meeting 85 percent of their quality standards would get two lemons. And, of course, it could go to three and four lemons (for the ones made on Monday morning) and finally to complete "rebuilds" (retentions). Or Chrysler could decide: "We have to improve the processes we use for making cars, and we need to design engines and vehicles that get better mileage so that all our vehicles will have no lemons on their window sticker."

Now let's take this comparison to a school district and look at hypothetical data that could well have emerged from implementing steps 1–5 above. Let's assume that the data indicate that some students aced the test, some did very well, the largest group was in the average category, some were below average, and some just didn't get it. It would be easy to just give them all "appropriate" grades and encourage them to try harder next time. But this district happens to be led by a quality leader who embraces feedback, change, and continuous improvement. She brings her professional teachers together to analyze the student performance data and finds that everyone sort of expected this. No big surprises. Her question to them is critical:

Why wasn't every student able to demonstrate the intended level of learning at the conclusion of this learning opportunity?

If the teachers in this group are truly professional, and we expect that they are, they will offer answers that open the door to step 6, and the performance improvement process can unfold from there.

Performance Role 12: Improving Organizational Performance

If leaders desire to get better performance (and who wouldn't?), they must determine what's causing them to get the performance they're getting. If the performance is unsatisfactory, they'll want to improve it. But if the performance is good, quality leaders will want to make it even better!

Logic has it that if we continue doing things the way we always have, we'll probably get about the same results we've always gotten. So, improving organizational performance is directly dependent on modifying the process of production to get higher-quality results. For educators this translates into changing/modifying student learning experiences and opportunities to get better learning results. Either some students learn more, or more students learn what we intended, or both.

What quality leaders acknowledge, accept, and *embrace* is that quality cannot be improved without improving the process—and "trying harder" doesn't qualify. Since processes are often constrained/limited/bound by formal structures, improvement is often linked to deep organizational changes, not simply to technical ones. And given that schools are boxed in by structure after structure, performance improvement will necessarily involve way more than "fixing the teachers." (We explain this in depth in chapters 1 and 5 of *Learning Communities 2.0.*)

So let's return to our hypothetical school district and the analysis of its feedback data. Remember, we're assuming that the teachers involved in this analysis know a great deal about how and why students learn. Therefore, they're likely to identify the following as probable causes underlying their results:

- Many of the students didn't have the prerequisite learnings. (Way back when, both Madeline Hunter and Benjamin Bloom taught us that the number one determiner of student learning success is whether or not students have the required prerequisite learnings. Yet our present school structure has teachers beginning their classes knowing that many do not have the required prerequisite learning.)

- Some would have probably scored better if they were given more time to learn and/or more time to complete the exam. (Everyone knows that students' learning rates differ, but how does the structure accommodate that reality?)

- Some were not interested in or motivated by the content we used to teach the lesson. (Yes, areas of interest and what individuals find to be meaningful vary enormously.)

These three statements are not just guesses. They are supported by some of our most basic research about students and learning, and every principal and teacher knows them. The question that this staff faces,

Profile of Service Leaders

Learning, living, and leading compassionately and with dedication . . . enabled by a highly developed EQ (emotional quotient)

The Gurus	Robert Greenleaf and Ken Blanchard
Exemplars	Mother Teresa and Paul Newman
Antithesis	Kenneth Lay (disgraced ex-Enron CEO)
Mind-Set	People are our most valuable asset, and they will do the "right thing right" if they get our consistent support.
Purpose	To support the change process by aligning the organization's policies, structures, and reward system with its vision
Focus	• Organizing to make the best use of *all* our resources • Utilizing the best in employee talents and skills • Serving the community; doing well by doing good
Change Belief	Change happens, and is sustained, when people are supported and rewarded for making vision-directed change.
Performance Roles	• Rewarding positive contributions • Restructuring to achieve results • Managing the organization's vision
Key Sources	• *Servant Leadership* (Robert Greenleaf, 1991) • *Leading at a Higher Level* (Ken Blanchard, 2006) • *The Element* (Ken Robinson, 2009) • *The Serving Leader* (Ken Jennings and John Stahl-Wert, 2004) • *The Power of Alignment* (George Labovitz and Victor Rosansky, 1997) • *Stewardship* (Peter Block, 1987, new edition 1993)

along with countless others like them in North America, is what will they actually *do* to address these three issues? What within the structure and process of their instructional system will they choose to change?

Our view is that they will not significantly improve their performance results or their learner outcomes until they replace the industrial age, assembly-line instructional delivery and opportunity structures of their schools. As we noted in chapter 3, a step in the right direction would be to embrace the power of transformational technology and use it to customize learning experiences and opportunities for their students—much as Apple did for the music industry and Amazon.com has done for book sales. Many other fruitful alternatives are described in depth throughout *Learning Communities 2.0*. But for now, let's simply acknowledge that technology, used correctly and creatively, has the power to eliminate the three reasons the teachers gave for the inadequate performance of more than half of the class. If we keep the industrial paradigm and assembly-line schools, we'll always have winners and losers, letter grades, and the bell curve.

Yet Toyota doesn't have, or need, a bell curve to evaluate its products. They long ago opted for skilled and empowered workers, feedback loops, and continuous improvement of their processes for doing things. Yes, we know, we know, we know, learners are more complex than cars—but that makes our case even more powerfully. Why should complex human beings be subjected to a standardized assembly-line structure, when there's nothing about a class of thirty students that is standardized except their age?

The point this raises, which quality leaders must openly confront, is that our present school structures severely limit the performance improvement options open to professional educators—particularly options that reflect what our professional teachers know about learning and learners. Maybe this is why some critics of our educational system are convinced that the term "educational change" is more oxymoron than reality.

The Essence of Service Leadership

The main thing is to keep the main thing the main thing!

—George Labovitz and Victor Rosansky

**Being keeper of the dream and keeper of the vision
is at the core of service leadership.**

Because Total Leadership is about creating and sustaining productive change, it cannot succeed without service leadership. Service leaders do everything possible to establish organizational support, the fifth and final pillar that underlies successful change efforts. They are masters at strategic alignment, which means that everything (and that means everything) that moves in the organization, and some that doesn't, has to be synced/ aligned/matched with the organization's strategic direction—its concrete picture of its ideal future. No friction allowed. If a person, a process, a practice, a procedure, or an organizational structure is rubbing against the smooth road toward fulfilling the vision, it must be corrected and smoothed. The path must be friction-free.

Service leaders focus on ensuring that this alignment take place, and they willingly support those committed to what the organization will look like, feel like, and be like when operating at its ideal best. In short, service leaders are in service to the organization's declared purpose and vision, and in service to those who are committed to and working toward that ideal future. And for the most part they carry out this role selflessly—no ego, applause, recognition, or special benefits required. The previous four TL2.0 leadership domains discuss how essential it is to have a reason to change, a clear picture of the change, commitment to the change, and the ability to make the change. But those changes won't happen, nor will they last, until the service leader enters the picture and closes the circle by establishing the direct organizational support that makes deep and lasting change possible.

If our description sounds more tough-minded than kindhearted, service leaders will be the first to say:

The compassionate and wise thing to do is to deal with issues directly and get to the bottom of problems, not ignore them.

To sidestep issues or people that impair the effectiveness of the organization and its members is no act of kindness for anyone.

Support is demonstrated by the organization's willingness and ability to put itself and its resources squarely behind its declared purpose and vision, and squarely behind the people it counts on to implement them. Support reflects TL2.0s' commitment to and involvement in the change process, specifically their willingness to make tough decisions, commit people and resources, and operate in potentially new and unfamiliar ways that align with organizational purpose and vision. Over the years we've said that service leaders are the people in the organization who do the heavy lifting, and we think that the redefining and restructuring of organizational roles and familiar ways of doing business is about as heavy as the lifting gets. We'll be illustrating the "heavy lifting" required in education throughout *Learning Communities 2.0*, so stay tuned for that.

When viewed from the perspective of the entire TL2.0 model, service leadership requires significant doses of the other four domains as well, since their success depends on their having the desire and ability to:

1. Ask organizational members what needs to be done to support their success

2. Cultivate their desire to contribute their best

3. Remove organizational obstacles to their doing so

4. Reward the contributions of those who step up and contribute

Translating Vision into Concrete Form

When organizations create their visions with the grounding and thoroughness suggested in chapters 5 and 6, service leaders have a good start toward translating what is a comprehensive verbal picture of the organization into tangible actions that can be implemented. But service leaders must also be skilled at operationalizing fuzzy concepts and operationalizing fuzzy visions—because they, too, abound. However, we have long argued that for visions to be powerful, they must be bold, they must be clear and concrete, and they must run well ahead of your present capacity to operationalize them. Furthermore, *everyone in the organization must understand his or her role in making the vision a reality if it is to happen.*

Our more successful clients have followed this advice and created verbal visions around the most important features of an ideal effective school system—one that directly supports the learning success of every student. Typically their vision statements address nine distinctive elements: the student experience, the curriculum, the instructional delivery system, student assessment, technology, the staff, leadership, facilities, and community support. The shaded box is an example of one system's vision from the "student experience" perspective.

The Silver City Student Experience Vision
What learning is like from a student's perspective

- I am very involved in planning my learning experiences. My learning coach from school and my parents get involved in helping me set my direction, but as I progress, I am becoming more responsible for my own learning program.
- Every day, I come to school and am met at my developmental learning level. I am challenged, I am usually very successful, and I leave school wanting to return tomorrow.
- All Silver City students are naturally highly motivated to learn because the learning experiences of each student are matched to his developmental learning level, his learning styles and strengths, and his interests.
- I learn in many ways—about one-half of my learning is online—and I also take part in numerous seminars with other learners. I attend large group lectures, I read a lot, and I learn from mentors in our community.
- Silver City students like me believe that today's world requires lifelong learners, so our teachers design learning activities to ensure that graduates leave our schools as self-directed, future-focused, lifelong learners. As I advance through my program, I increasingly become accountable for my own learning.
- I have an electronic learner outcome portfolio that contains a complete record of my learning accomplishments. My parents, my learning coach, and my teachers all have access to my portfolio.

This bold and clear student experience vision is consistent with the "mass customized learning" vision that will be described in more detail in chapter 6 of *Learning Communities 2.0*. It's only one of eight statements for this anonymous school system, but it illustrates the challenge and opportunity that districts like this face. Vision statements with this level of specificity facilitate the more detailed plans that must be created by the leadership team, the curriculum and instruction department, the technology department, food service, transportation, and everyone else in the system.

The Moral Foundation of Service Leaders

Service leaders operate from a moral foundation that places risk taking and teamwork at the pinnacle of their core values chart. These values are manifested in their commitment to two particular principles of professionalism: alignment and contribution.

- **Risk Taking**. Service leaders know that change, innovation, and restructuring demand creativity, courage, tenacity, and a willingness to fail. Not everything goes right on the first try.

- **Teamwork**. Service leaders are team players, willing to play the roles of listener, contributor, supporter, and resource provider.

- **Alignment**. Alignment might be the title of the service leader's job description. If the request moves us toward the vision, their response is "Yes." If it doesn't move us toward the vision, it's "Sorry."

- **Contribution**. Service leaders have a *big* stake in the vision. They will do what it takes to make it happen . . . selflessly . . . even when no one is watching.

The Critical Performance Roles of Service Leaders

Service leadership is shaped through consistent attention to three critical performance roles, each of which helps drive organizational alignment:

- Rewarding positive contributions (and . . .)

- Restructuring to achieve results (as key elements in . . .)

- Managing the organization's vision

Here's what they look like in action.

Performance Role 13: Rewarding Positive Contributions

Education is a people business. Our greatest assets *really are* our people. For service leaders, "People are our greatest asset" is not a slogan; it's a reality. People-oriented organizations thrive when they can attract, hire, and retain creative, talented, and responsible people. Daniel Pink in *A Whole New Mind* and Richard Florida in *The Flight of the Creative Class* tell us about how necessary it is today to employ people who are creative and talented. They also tell us how difficult it is to keep them. TL2.0s no longer hire people who are simply "qualified;" they seek out and select those who are "uniquely talented." In short, service leaders continually seek more effective ways to attract, hire, and retain good people.

It is quite natural for people to do what they get rewarded for doing, and that reward can be something tangible like dollars or something intangible like feeling appreciated. Service leaders are fully aware of this and use both tangible and intangible rewards to keep their team enthused, motivated, and engaged. But they do not simply reward people for their enthusiasm, motivation, and engagement, but for contributions that are aligned with and directly support the organization's inspirational vision. In doing so, service leaders do their best to align three powerful forces that bolster productive engagement: (1) the personal values of individuals, (2) the core values of the team and the organization, and (3) the rewards they control. Aligning these three motivators assures them of having team members who are both engaged and productive.

In *First, Break All the Rules*, Marcus Buckingham and Curt Coffman identify what their research has shown to be "the core elements needed to attract, focus, and keep the most talented employees." They're all cost free . . . and expect some surprises. (We love number 10, but wait until you get there!) Here they are:

1. Do I know what is expected of me at work?

2. Do I have the materials and equipment I need to do my work right?

3. At work, do I have the opportunity to do what I do best every day?

4. In the last seven days, have I received recognition or praise for good work?

5. Does my supervisor, or someone at work, seem to care about me as a person?

6. Is there someone at work who encourages my development?

7. At work, do my opinions seem to count?

8. Does the mission/purpose of my company make me feel like my work is important?

9. Are my coworkers committed to doing quality work?

10. Do I have a best friend at work?

11. In the last six months, have I talked with someone about my progress?

12. At work, have I had opportunities to learn and grow?

These simply stated questions summarize much of what the literature tells us are the "soft" and powerful motivators that foster meaningful work, engagement, and production. And, we repeat, they don't cost money! However, we must be quick to add that all of these soft motivators lose their power when salaries, benefits, and perks are not competitive with the market. Therefore, it's better to think, "We must pay to get the best, the creative, the talented. But that by itself isn't enough. Once we get them, these twelve soft rewards are what maximize our dollar investment." Since education leaders aren't in a position to entice high performance with discretionary bonuses, we think they'd benefit enormously from consciously, openly, and skillfully acting on these twelve important elements of engagement—and creating expectations that everyone else in the organization should and will, too.

Positive Contributions

If service leaders are to reward positive contributions, they must first be able to spot them. Specifically, service leaders look for contributions consistent with and aligned with the organization's declared values, mission, vision, and intended results. You won't be surprised by some of the following contributions, but others are new and highly relevant in today's age of empowerment:

- **Hard work**. Who's doing the heavy lifting around here? Yes, it's a bit old-fashioned, but hard work is still hard work, and not everyone seeks it out!

- **Risk taking and winning**. Risk taking and winning happen when we plan well and everything comes together. This powerful combination usually leads to breakthroughs that pave the way for future success.

- **Risk taking, losing, and learning**. Our culture has taught us to fear the concept of losing. But losing is a setback and an opportunity to learn. If a leader has never failed, it's obvious that he or she hasn't taken the risks necessary to significantly improve.

- **Committing fully in team efforts**. Attention, please! We have a new cultural icon: The Lone Ranger has been replaced by the staff of *ER*, with the Los Angeles Lakers coming in a close second! (Quickly now, in ten seconds or less, name the Lone Ranger's horse, his sidekick, and his sidekick's horse. If you get all three right, consider yourself past your prime . . . because your staff already does!)

- **Challenges to the status quo**. It takes courage to take on city hall . . . or the state capitol. That's why most choose to blend in with the norms of the organization. But telling people in authority that they "have no clothes on" is sometimes what's needed to keep the organization on track and improving.

- **Doing it on time, with quality, *and* a smile**. Most good organizations, including schools, are privileged to employ a number of people who continue to do what is expected, with superior quality, and in the process, make the organization a better place for everyone.

- **The natural**. Some people just seem to win more often than others. They are naturals who just seem to have it, to always be in their element. We need to reward those naturals, who sometimes work hard but *always* seem to work smart.

Rewards are only rewards if they are perceived to be rewards by the intended "rewardee." Yes, like Shakespeare's "beauty," rewards are in the eyes and heart of the beholder. So when service leaders are unsure of how people like to be rewarded for their contributions, they ask them. Invariably, employees begin by talking about money as the ultimate reward, but service leaders know that everyone likes money. And they also know that money isn't a very good long-term motivator, especially for someone whose basic needs are already being met. That's why they keep the above list of soft motivators handy. Receiving a raise usually makes employees feel good for a week or two, but then it's back to business as usual. However, when the raise comes directly from an influential supervisor, and with a short speech about the value of the employee's contribution and a pat on the back, it takes on a far more powerful symbolic and motivational value. Chances are, in fact, that the speech and the pat are of far greater value than the dollars that accompanied them.

Rewarding with Powerful Motivators and Messages

Using the following powerful motivators and messages can encourage people to work at their creative and productive best.

The Motivator	The Message
Recognition	We want others to know about your success.
Advancement	Let us help you with your career path.
Freedom	You set the agenda . . . we'll get the resources.
Responsibility	This is big . . . and we need you to do it.
Attagirls/Attaboys	Way to go! I saw and appreciate what you did.
Influence	We want you to help us make our big, important decisions.
Dollars	This organization shares the rewards of its success.

Clearly, then, service leaders recognize that the most powerful motivators are free. They work to pay fair salaries and provide fair benefits, and they lobby their organization to enhance the welfare of their people. But beyond that, they work through the motivators of opportunity, influence, freedom, responsibility, recognition, and empowerment to bring new purposes, visions, and possibilities into tangible form.

Performance Role 14: Restructuring to Achieve Results

The term "restructuring" has become a buzzword and has come to mean almost anything that has to do with change of any kind, whether the change is as trivial as technical tinkering or as profound as paradigm transformation. As we will demonstrate in detail in chapter 1 of *Learning Communities 2.0*, we profoundly disagree with all "casual" interpretations of restructuring. As a reminder, let's venture back to the final section of chapter 2, where we described the prevailing operating structure of most schools today:

> Specific students of a specific age must learn specific things on a specific schedule in a specific classroom from a specific teacher using specific materials and methods so that they can pass specific tests on specific dates—and only then be called "OK."

If you know anyone who thinks that a casual effort at "restructuring" this entrenched pattern will bring about significant change, please give him or her your copy of this book, and we'll send you a new one free.

Service leaders, by contrast, focus on restructuring that creates alignment between the organization's vision and its structure—its pattern of action and "way of doing business." And they do so knowing that

- A structure is a tangible, fundamental pattern of organizational action; you can see it and/or watch it.

- Structures are created to accomplish specific organizational ends.

- Structures can be bureaucratic, controlling, and designed for administrative convenience (like the one above), or they can be flexible and client-centered (read "learner-centered").

- Structures that make sense for accomplishing a given end/outcome usually will not work effectively if that end/outcome changes.

- Structures can take on a life of their own, known as institutional inertia, which makes achieving new ends very difficult. For example, the assembly-line instructional delivery structure described above makes customizing learning nearly impossible.

From what we described in chapter 6, service leaders in education are going to be working with an organizational purpose and vision that are going to require a structure that promotes something much closer to this:

Anyone can learn anything at anytime from anywhere from world-class experts using the most transformational technologies and resources available to enhance his or her personal interests and life fulfillment.

And that's going to require service leaders to ignore the old truism "Form follows function" and embrace a new one: "Form follows vision." Until the new vision has been identified, defined, described, and committed to, of course, there is no way to know what kind of organizational structure will best facilitate it. But we're willing to bet that it will come pretty close to this latter one.

So let's consolidate all of the above with what we've learned over time about this fourteenth performance role into what for us have become two basic truths, namely:

1. If the structure of the organization doesn't change, don't expect the roles and behaviors of the organization's members to change. Service leaders must see this connection if they're to successfully support and implement the new vision.

2. If a school system doesn't replace the industrial age assembly-line delivery of instruction with something that allows for learner-centered customization, the impact of its change effort will be no more than tinkering. Making the change to a customized instructional delivery system is a paradigm shift requiring risk taking of the first order, as implied above.

Because they inherently begin with the end in mind, service leaders use purpose and vision as both their starting point and their bottom line. By designing back from where they want to end up, they approach their work with a perspective that is revolutionary to those accustomed to starting with the present and planning forward. For service leaders, there is only one place to start: the organization's top priority. That means having all students demonstrate the district's exit outcomes successfully. And if you accept that students learn at different rates and in different ways, the bureaucratic, Industrial Age, assembly line of instruction and credentialing both have to go. They can't be oiled, painted, added to, or renamed. The assembly line is a structure that was right for an earlier era, but that era is long past.

Performance Role 15: Managing the Organization's Vision

Without immediate, enthusiastic, and visible support from leaders and leadership teams, a newly formed compelling purpose and vision will have the shelf life of a ripe banana. Why? Because after that stimulating meeting in which people create an exciting reason for being, and picture a perfect organizational future, they return to their same old offices the next morning. The people they meet on their way into the office are the same people they left the day before; the people waiting outside their office don't even know they have this new vision; the mail in their in-boxes was sent before the vision was drafted; and their desk and surroundings look just like they did when they left.

It's reality time! And that's why we began our description of service leadership with this powerful quote from Labovitz and Rosansky:

The main thing is to keep the main thing the main thing!

In fact, it's one of our favorite quotes of all time—and for good reason. "Institutional inertia" and its first cousin, "cultural inertia," are incredibly powerful and will undermine the best of change efforts—pillars and all.

So before that inspiring meeting ends and the authentic and visionary leaders send all the participants out the door, the service leader must leap to his or her feet and announce:

I'll be dropping by each of your offices several times tomorrow, offering suggestions about how we can make *our* new main thing *your* new main thing and sustain the enthusiasm and momentum we've built these last few days. I've already cleared my schedule so that I could spend the time with you, and we'll just keep on keeping on together with this strategic design until our vision that's now on paper becomes our organizational reality. Have a good evening, and see you tomorrow!

What a brilliant, and necessary, move! If the service leader had simply let people return to their offices and confront the old pile of things that were marked "urgent" prior to strategic design, their enthusiasm and momentum would quickly dissipate, and the district would soon be kissing their new strategic design good-bye. Framing the vision is one thing; keeping and managing it is another. And that's what service leaders were born to do.

But there's more. Good old inertia will continue to raise its familiar head, over and over again—often as confusion and uncertainty, but inevitably as resistance. So this is exactly why service leaders must be more than its match and know that it's inevitably coming at them. And when it does, the "heavy lifting" aspect of Total Leadership really begins.

Since their whole agenda is about alignment, savvy service leaders know that their work is challenging, but doable. This means giving continual attention to five key things that can either be assets or liabilities in keeping the main thing the main thing: structures, policies, processes, practices, and people. All are important, but people and structures are the most critical and most difficult. Here are the four that we haven't already addressed.

Policies

New visions, if bold, require establishing new priorities and new policies (both written and unwritten) and abandoning some long-established ways of doing business. For example, if a vision is for everyone to be empowered and encouraged to improve, but the staff evaluation policy embodies a deficit model that punishes people for unsatisfactory performance and doesn't promote development and empowerment, it has to go.

Processes

The way a leader effectively operated in the past is probably aligned with an old, outdated vision, not one that is bold and future-focused. For example, a principal may have previously hired a teacher because he or she thought the teacher would be "good." But now, the principal has embraced the idea that all students can learn well, and that having students learn something well is more important than when they learn it. To bring the selection process and practices in line with these new beliefs, the principal will have to establish a process that results in hiring not just good teachers, but good teachers whose beliefs and intentions are consistent with the new vision.

Practices

The common practices that need alignment may be the most difficult to identify, and they are usually unwritten. For instance, "successful" practices for supervising the lunchroom may be authoritarian and controlling, while the new vision may emphasize students taking control of their own behavior. This conflict may require training the aides who supervise the lunch hall in a different approach. Service leaders must be particularly sensitive to non-alignments of this kind, since they're probably not covered in the policy manual.

People

Everyone in the organization needs to implement the new vision. If only those who find the new vision comfortable or exciting implement it, then creating and sustaining productive change will be impossible. That is why implementing the organization's vision must become the key role and goal of every supervisor in the system. Service leaders make supporting and monitoring the implementation of the vision the central part of the supervision process. And they can certainly clearly signal that the organization's purpose and vision are important and real when each supervision session begins with

**Tell me about the things you are doing that are
helping us to put our vision into practice.**

We believe strongly that dialogue-initiating questions such as these need to be asked at every level of the organization, starting with the school board's evaluation session with the superintendent. And to bolster our conviction, we've created a "supervision for alignment" process that features a dozen dialogue-starting statements that penetrate to the core of the strategic design process and its ultimate implementation in schools and classrooms. The process is being systematically used in a number of school districts that recognize how important a proactive process of this nature is to creating "people alignment."

EPILOGUE

ep•i•logue   a conclusion to what has happened
(We looked it up.)

Everyone who has ever written about leadership seems to have a favorite definition for the word, for the act, for the process. When we each started thinking seriously about leadership as a field of study thirty years ago, we defined leadership simply as "influence." Leadership was the act and/or process of "influencing others." We now have extended that definition quite a bit. Given the rapid nature of change in today's world, and the wellsprings from which leaders operate, we now define the word as follows:

lead•er•ship   future-focused, heartfelt influence

Leadership is future-focused, heartfelt influence. Given this definition of leadership, the TL2.0 leadership framework and the core of this book can be used anywhere and everywhere to achieve change about anything. Leadership is a deeply motivated and directed activity, to accomplish a goal. TL2.0s without a meaningful goal or vision are like Corvettes sitting idling—all kinds of potential energy raring to go, but without the catalyst to make it kinetic.

Education Through Leadership Eyes

The TL framework is not an "educational leadership" framework. *TL2.0* is actually a leadership book that happens to contain many educational examples. But it could just as well have been a leadership book that contained many business examples, or many athletic coaching examples, or many "not-for-profit" examples, or—dreaded thought—even many visionary crime examples. (Please don't tell anyone that we said that, OK?) This is true because the framework was built from universal examples, and it applies "right back" in that universal way.

When we reflect on our work of the past decade, we have come to believe that the acceptance of *Total Leaders* was due to its being one of the first/only books to encourage educational leaders to look at education through "leadership eyes . . . and through leadership glasses." Other educational leadership books nearly universally ask educators to look at leadership through the tired eyes of all-too-familiar educational issues.

For example, this approach gets us first thinking about "what can we do to increase student achievement?" or whatever issue is on our mind; then we look at leadership opportunities through our "lack of student achievement" glasses. For us, the TL2.0 framework is like riding a bike and enjoying the wide beautiful panoramic view of the scenic highway, rather than riding in a car and craning your neck to see a specific scene through your windshield. (This analogy works even better if you can remember the limited view you had in those old cars with their flat, small windshields. Well, if you're not old enough to remember them, we sure are.)

So now that you're a bona fide TL2.0 leader with all the knowledge, understandings, insights, and skills from all those famous leadership gurus . . . *so what?* ("So what?" is our favorite question because it always takes us to a deeper level of purpose.) SO WHAT!? (You'll note that we are shouting now.) SO WHAT are you going to do with all these new resources? Well, our intent is that you use your new expertise, new competence, and new commitment to transform education. And one of the best ways to apply your newfound knowledge and skills is to operationalize the vision that you'll find in *TL2.0*'s companion book, *Learning Communities 2.0*.

Although we've written *TL2.0* and *LC2.0* to be stand-alone books, each was written with the key elements of the other clearly in mind. You can read and learn from each without having to read the other, but they are companion books. They share many common elements, and they complement each other. Hence, you'll find synergy in reading both. *TL2.0* is about leadership and *LC2.0* is about using those leadership skills and insights to create empowerment age learning communities—learning communities unlocked from the old, tired, content-driven curriculum of the past, and unlocked from the totally outdated assembly-line instructional delivery system of the industrial age. In short, *TL2.0* draws on the latest and best about leadership, and *LC2.0* draws on the latest and best about what twenty-first-century education could and should be.

Our Heartfelt Thanks

On our good hair days we tend to be rather humble guys—which is why we start most of our workshops by thanking participants for giving us their time and the opportunity to influence them. For us, those are gifts, gifts of high value. Time is a nonrenewable resource—we each get exactly twenty-four hours per day. And openness to influence is taking the risk that your deep beliefs and values will be challenged. This also applies, of course, when you take the time to read *TL2.0* and allow us to challenge your beliefs and values regarding leadership, change, and education. Thank you . . . a sincere thank-you! It is an honor to reach into the lives and work of so many wonderful people this way.

Our Friendly Advice

. . . offered at no extra charge. So take heed as we ride off into the sunset on our white horses into Empowermentland, and before you look at those two silver bullets and say, "Who were those masked men, anyway?" here are some parting thoughts that you're free to take as friendly advice if you care to.

Leadership indeed is "future-focused, heartfelt influence." Given that truism, that reality, what does it take for people to open themselves to be influenced? We think it's open minds and open hearts! *TL2.0* focused on leadership, on leadership domains, leadership performance roles, and leadership activities—all calibrated to resonate with the five pillars of change. But before all of that works to the optimum, openness to being influenced comes down to who you are and the relationship that you've established with each person you are attempting to influence. And that relationship is based on

- **Trust**. Does this person attempting to influence me have my best interests in mind? Or am I being manipulated for his or her ends? Trust is a historical concept based on behaviors. We gain trust over time by how we treat other people.

- **A Track Record**. Where have you been and what have you done that has clearly benefited others? What is your reputation? What is your "brand?" How have you behaved when you won? And when you lost? People open to our influence when we have a winning record and have helped others in the process.

- **Logic/Rationale**. Simply pleading "trust me" doesn't work well unless you make sense. Effective changeleaders (yes, one word) articulate a logical and solid rationale for what needs to happen and why it needs to happen. Using Anthony Gregoric's terms, they're "concrete sequentials" when explaining what and why, and they're "abstract randoms" when dreaming and visioning about what could be.

- **Usability and Doability**. People listen when new ideas with the potential to solve problems are presented. People don't take risks when the risks aren't worth the potential rewards. Visions are often tricky to sell. Leaders must simultaneously take people to places they've never been before, while painting a picture that looks and feels "doable."

- **Rings with Reality**. Does the leader's description of reality, of future conditions, of opportunities and challenges ring true for those he or she is attempting to influence? If a mutual sense of reality is not achieved, any attempts at influence will not gain traction.

- **Pulls at the Heartstrings**. Compelling purposes and inspiring visions stir the soul. That's the real source of motivation for most people, and it's the key to tapping the wellsprings of empowerment so badly needed in today's complex and challenging world.

- **From Theory to Practice**. To effective leaders, good theories *are* practical. They point the direction to informed practice. Effective changeleaders must create visions based on sound research and potentially paradigm-shifting theories, but they must also be convincing when describing how that theory will look when we're doing it. If that sounds a lot like making a vision concrete, it should.

So join us as we now move from *TL2.0* to *LC2.0*! Hi-yo, Silver! *Away!*

SUPPORTING RESOURCES

Ambrose, D. (2003). *Leadership: The Journey Inward.* Dubuque, IA: Kendall/Hunt Publishing Company.

Anderson, C. (2008). *The Long Tail.* New York: Hyperion.

———. (2009). *Free,* New York: Hyperion.

Barker, J. (1988). *Discovering the Future: The Business of Paradigms.* St. Paul, MN: ILI Press.

Beck, D., and C. Cowan. (1996). *Spiral Dynamics.* Malden, MA: Blackwell.

Bennis, W., D. Goleman, and J. O'Toole. (2008). *Transparency.* San Francisco: Jossey-Bass.

Bennis, W., and B. Nanus. (1985). *Leaders: Strategies for Taking Charge.* New York: Harper & Row.

Blanchard, K. (2007). *Leading at a Higher Level.* Upper Saddle River, NJ: Prentice Hall.

Blanchard, K., and J. Britt. (2009). *Who Killed Change?* New York: HarperCollins.

Blanchard, K., and N. V. Peale. (1988). *The Power of Ethical Management.* New York: Morrow.

Blanchard, K., and G. Ridge. (2009). *Helping People Win at Work.* Upper Saddle River, NJ: FT Press.

Block, P. (1993). *Stewardship.* San Francisco: Berrett-Koehler.

Bogle, J. (2009). *Enough: True Measures of Money, Business, and Life.* Hoboken, NJ: Wiley.

Bossidy, L., and R. Charan. (2002). *Execution: The Discipline of Getting Things Done.* New York: Crown Business.

———. (2004). *Confronting Reality.* New York: Crown Business.

Braden, G. (2008). *The Spontaneous Healing of Belief.* Carlsbad, CA: Hay House.

Brafman, O., and R. Beckstrom. (2006). *The Starfish and the Spider.* London: Penguin Group.

Bridges, W. (1991). *Managing Transitions.* Reading, MA: Addison-Wesley.

Buckingham, M. (2005). *The One Thing You Need to Know about Great Managing, Great Leading, and Sustained Individual Success.* New York: Free Press.

Buckingham, M., and D. Clifton. (2001). *Now, Discover Your Strengths.* New York: Free Press.

Buckingham, M., and C. Coffman. (1999). *First, Break All the Rules.* New York: Simon & Schuster.

Carter, S. (1996). *Integrity.* New York: HarperCollins.

Christensen, C., S. Anthony, and E. Roth. (2004). *Seeing What's Next.* Boston: Harvard Business School Publishing.

Collins, J. (2001). *Good to Great.* New York: HarperCollins.

Cooper, R., and A. Sawaf. (1997). *Executive EQ.* New York: Penguin Putnam.

Covert, J., and T. Satterson. (2009). *The One Hundred Best Business Books of All Time.* New York: Penguin.

Covey, S. M. R. (2006). *The Speed of Trust.* New York: Free Press.

Covey, S. R. (1989). *The Seven Habits of Highly Effective People.* New York: Simon & Schuster.

———. (1991). *Principle-Centered Leadership.* New York: Summit Books.

———. (2004). *The Eighth Habit: From Effectiveness to Greatness.* New York: Free Press.

Deming, W. E. (1986). *Out of the Crisis.* Cambridge, MA: MIT Press.

Dyer, W. (2004). *The Power of Intention.* Carlsbad, CA: Hay House.

Farber, S. (2009). *Greater Than Yourself.* New York: Doubleday.

Ferriss, T. (2007). *The Four-Hour Workweek.* New York: Crown.

Fleming, J., and J. Asplund. (2007). *Human Sigma.* New York: Gallup Press.

Florida, R. (2005). *The Flight of the Creative Class.* New York: HarperCollins.

Friedman, G. (2009). *The Next 100 Years.* New York: Doubleday.

Friedman, T. (2005). *The World Is Flat.* New York: Farrar, Straus & Giroux.

——— (2008). *Hot, Flat, and Crowded.* New York: Farrar, Straus & Giroux.

Gardner, H. (2004). *Changing Minds.* Boston: Harvard Business School Press.

———. (2006). *Five Minds for the Future.* Boston: Harvard Business School Press.

George, B., with P. Sims. (2007). *True North.* San Francisco: Jossey-Bass.

Gittell, J. (2003). *The Southwest Airlines Way.* New York: McGraw-Hill.

Goldsmith, M. (2007). *What Got You Here Won't Get You There.* New York: Hyperion.

Goleman, D. (1995). *Emotional Intelligence.* New York: Bantam Books.

———. (1998). *Working with Emotional Intelligence.* New York: Bantam Books.

———. (2006). *Social Intelligence.* New York: Bantam Dell.

———. (2009). *Ecological Intelligence.* New York: Random House.

Goleman, D., R. Boyatzis, and A. McKee. (2002). *Primal Leadership.* Boston: Harvard Business School Press.

Greenleaf, R. (1991). *Servant Leadership.* New York: Paulist Press.

Hamel, G., and C. K. Prahalad. (1994). *Competing for the Future.* Boston: Harvard Business School Press.

Hawkins, D. R. (1995). *Power vs. Force.* Carlsbad, CA: Hay House.

Hicks, E., and J. Hicks. (2006). *The Amazing Power of Deliberate Intent.* Carlsbad, CA: Hay House.

Holmes, E. (2005). *How to Use the Science of Mind.* Burbank, CA: Science of Mind Publishing.

Jennings, K., and J. Stahl-Wert. (2004). *The Serving Leader.* San Francisco: Berrett-Koehler.

Kaplan, R., and D. Norton. (1996). *The Balanced Scorecard.* Boston: Harvard Business School Press.

Kessler, R. (2000). *The Soul of Education.* Alexandria, VA: Association for Supervision and Curriculum Development.

Kotter, J. P. (1996). *Leading Change.* Boston: Harvard Business School Press.

———. (2008). *A Sense of Urgency.* Boston: Harvard Business School Press.

Kouzes, J., and B. Posner. (2003). *Credibility.* San Francisco: Jossey-Bass.

Labovitz, G., and V. Rosansky. (1997). *The Power of Alignment.* New York: Wiley.

Liedtka, J., R. Rosen, and R. Wiltbank. (2009). *The Catalyst.* New York: Crown Business.

Lipton, B. (2005). *The Biology of Belief.* Carlsbad, CA: Hay House.

Negroponte, N. (1995). *Being Digital.* New York: Knopf.

O'Toole, J., and E. Lawler III. (2006). *The New American Workplace.* New York: Palgrave Macmillan.

Palfrey, J., and U. Glasser. (2008). *Born Digital.* New York: Basic Books.

Penn, M. (2007). *Microtrends.* New York: Hachette.

Peters, T. (1997). *The Circle of Innovation.* New York: Knopf.

———. (2003). *Re-Imagine!* London: Dorling Kindersley.

———. (2005). *Design.* New York: Dorling Kindersley.

Pink, D. (2001). *Free Agent Nation.* New York: Warner Books.

———. (2005). *A Whole New Mind.* New York: Riverhead Books.

———. (2009). *Drive.* New York: Riverhead Books.

Poscente, V. (2008). *The Age of Speed.* Austin, TX: Bard Press.

Rath, T., and D. Clifton. (2004). *How Full Is Your Bucket?* New York: Gallup Press.

Rath, T., and B. Conchie. (2008). *Strengths-Based Leadership*. New York: Gallup Press.

Robinson, K. (2009). *The Element: How Finding Your Passion Changes Everything*. New York: Viking.

Schwahn, C. J. (1993). *Making Change Happen: An Action-Planning Handbook*. Dillon, CO: Breakthrough Learning Systems.

Schwahn, C. J., and W. G. Spady. (1998). *Total Leaders*. Arlington, VA: American Association of School Administrators.

Senge, P. (1990). *The Fifth Discipline*. New York: Doubleday.

Shirky, C. (2008). *Here Comes Everybody*. New York: Penguin.

Sounds True. (2008). *Measuring the Immeasurable*. Boulder, CO: Sounds True Inc.

Spady, W. G. (1994). *Outcome-Based Education: Critical Issues and Answers*. Arlington, VA: American Association of School Administrators.

———. (1998). *Paradigm Lost: Reclaiming America's Educational Future*. Arlington, VA: American Association of School Administrators.

———. (2001). *Beyond Counterfeit Reforms*. Boston: Scarecrow Press.

Spady, W. G., and C. J. Schwahn. (2010). *Learning Communities 2.0*. Lanham, MD: Rowman & Littlefield.

Studer, Q. (2004). *Hardwiring Excellence*. Gulf Breeze, FL: Fire Starter Publishing.

Surowiecki, J. (2005). *The Wisdom of Crowds*. New York: Anchor Books.

Tapscott, D., and A. Williams. (2006). *Wikinomics: How Mass Collaboration Changes Everything*. London: Penguin.

Theobald, R. (1987). *The Rapids of Change*. Indianapolis, IN: Knowledge Systems.

Tolle, E. (1999). *Practicing the Power of Now*. Novato, CA: New World Library.

———. (2005). *A New Earth: Awakening to Your Life's Purpose*. London: Penguin.

Walsch, N. D. (2002). *The New Revelations*. New York: Atria Books.

———. (2004). *Tomorrow's God*. London: Hodder and Stoughton, Ltd.

———. (2009). *When Everything Changes, Change Everything*. Ashland, OR: EmNin Books.

Walton, M. (1986). *The Deming Management Method*. New York: Perigree Books.

Weinberger, D. (2007). *Everything Is Miscellaneous*. New York: Times Books.

Welch, J., and S. Welch. (2005). *Winning*. New York: HarperCollins.

Wilber, K. (2000). *A Theory of Everything*. Boston: Shambhala.

Wooden, J. (2005). *Wooden on Leadership*. New York: McGraw-Hill.

ABOUT THE AUTHORS

Charles J. Schwahn has made his professional life a study of leadership and effective organizations. For the past thirty years he has worked with businesses and school systems throughout North America providing consultation on the topics of leadership, change, and future-focused strategic design. His career has placed him in nearly all of the critical roles of the education profession, and his last "real" job was as superintendent of the Eagle County School District in Vail, Colorado. Chuck received his doctorate from the University of Massachusetts, where Ken Blanchard, of *The One-Minute Manager* fame, was his doctoral chair. Chuck and his wife Genny spend their summers in the Black Hills of South Dakota and winters in the Phoenix area. He can be reached at chuckschwahn@yahoo .com.

William G. Spady is the author of seven books and an internationally recognized authority on future-focused approaches to outcome-based education, organizational change, transformational leadership development, strategic organizational design, and empowering models of learning and living. For more than forty years he has spearheaded major efforts throughout North America, South Africa, and Australia on expanding the vision, deepening the philosophical grounding, and improving the performance of educators, leaders, educational systems, and learners of all ages in business and the public sector. He loves classical music, skiing, bicycling, scuba diving, walking in nature, and reading anything that expands his awareness and deepens his spirituality. He can be reached at billspady@earthlink.net.

CPSIA information can be obtained at www.ICGtesting.com
Printed in the USA
BVOW071605130512

290032BV00003B/5/P